TAHD
AL-AKHLĀQ

A Ḥadīth Guide
for personal and Social Conduct

Sayyed 'Abdu'l-Ḥayy al-Ḥasanī

UK ISLAMIC ACADEMY

First published in English by UK Islamic Academy,
P.O. Box 6645, Leicester LE5 5WT, UK

General Editor: Iqbal Ahmad Azami

ISBN 1 872531 19 9 (HB)
ISBN 1 872531 20 2 (PB)

British Library Cataloguing-in-Publication Data
A catalogue record for this book is available from the British Library

Typeset by: N.A. Qaddoura
Cover design: Imtiaze A. Manjra

Printed by: Interprint Ltd., Malta

CONTENTS

بسم الله الرحمن الرحيم

In the name of Allah, the Merciful, the Compassionate

FOREWORD

It is with thanks and praise to Allah ﷻ that the Islamic Academy has the opportunity to present Maulana Sayyed 'Abdu'l-Ḥayy al-Ḥasani's '*Tahdhīb al-Akhlāq: A Ḥadīth Guide for Personal and Social Conduct*'. During his lifetime the Maulana collected a selection of *aḥādīth* in small notebooks, but these were not published until after his death and then thanks to the efforts of his noble son, Sayyed Abul Hasan Ali Nadwi. Essentially, this collection of *aḥādīth* aims to be relevant to today's society and world and also act as an introduction to this science for students in their initial stages of Islamic education.

The task of refining behaviour and purifying the heart occupied one of the main objectives of the Prophet Muḥammad's mission. Wisdom manifests itself in good character and in good manners, and the Qur'an itself uses the term 'wisdom' to denote these traits. As is stated in one *ḥadīth*: "If there is no good character there is no wisdom. If there is no wisdom there is no good character." In attaining good character and wisdom, disciplining of the lower self is an essential ingredient, just as purifying one's heart. As the Prophet ﷺ said: "I was only sent to perfect good character."

Indeed there is no better exemplar of morality and good manners than the Prophet ﷺ, and his reported sayings and practices are but a guiding light for all Muslims: "Actions are only according to intentions. And everyone obtains what he intends." To follow the *ḥadīth* is to discipline oneself, to free oneself of affectation, vice, blameworthy attributes and deceptions; in short, to rid oneself of base characteristics and destructive habits. To practice what is learned from the *ḥadīth* is to achieve good manners and good character, to refine behaviour and purify the heart: "Allah does not look at your bodies or your forms; He looks at your hearts." Only through the cultivation of such qualities can wisdom be expressed.

Tahdhīb al-Akhlāq is divided into forty-five chapters; each chapter deals with the *ḥadīth* of various Traditionalists on issues ranging from *tawḥīd*, to earning a living, the treatment of animals, of neighbours, of one's family, modesty, *taqwa* and supplication. Most chapters are preceded by relevant *āyāts* from the Qur'ān and these reveal how the *ḥadīth* mirror Qur'anic teachings; "Anyone who introduces an innovation in this affair of ours which is not part of it, it will be rejected." All in all the Maulana's collection answers the most pertinent questions of the day, for example, on respecting one's parent, on work, contracts and obligations, moderation in all things and keeping good company: "Abandon that which gives you doubt for that which gives you no doubt." To read these *aḥādīth*, to understand them and put them into practice is to set oneself up, morally and spiritually, for life. In this way then the *aḥādīth* become religious knowledge and prophetic medicine.

Anyone who wishes to seek knowledge of the *dīn* will benefit greatly from *Tahdhīb al-Akhlāq* as in this short volume the goals of the prophetic mission are fulfilled: namely, refining character, purifying the heart and striving to reach total submission to Allah: "The greatness of the reward is from the greatness of the trial. When Allah, Exalted is He, loves a person, He tests them." In this respect, these *aḥādīth* aid the cleansing of the outward and the inward and serve to guide people on the path of salvation.

I would like to thank sister Aisha Bewley, brother Yacub Johnson, Abu Mustafa, Sarah Moore, my daughter Su'ad and all those who have participated in the production of this volume. May Allah reward all of them and accept this work from us and make it a source of guidance for Muslims the world over.

Leicester, UK
Rabīʿ al-Awwal 1424 AH

Iqbal Ahmad Azami

INTRODUCTION

Praise belongs to Allah, the Lord of the worlds, and peace be upon the noblest of the Messengers and the Seal of the Prophets, Muḥammad, the pure, the good, the truthful and trustworthy, and upon his family and his excellent Companions, and those who follow them in doing good until the Day of Repayment.

Allah Most High has mentioned the main goals of the mission of Muḥammad ﷺ, and its principal benefits in the same manner in each of four verses of the Wise Qur'ān. He ﷾ mentions the supplication of His intimate friend Ibrāhīm, peace be upon him, the ancestor of the Prophet ﷺ, the founder of the naturally monotheistic (*ḥanīf*) religion, and the one at whose hand the construction of the House was completed: *"Our Lord! Send amongst them a Messenger of their own who shall rehearse Thy Signs to them and instruct them in Scripture and Wisdom, and purify them. For Thou art the Exalted in Might, the Wise."* (2: 129) He ﷾ mentions these goals and benefits in the same way in a display of His generosity and a reminder of His blessings, saying: *"A similar (favour have ye already received) in that We have sent among you a Messenger of your own, rehearsing to you Our Signs, and purifying you, and instructing you in Scripture and Wisdom, and teaching you what you did not know. Then do ye remember Me; I will remember you. Be grateful to Me and reject not faith."* (2: 151–152) He ﷾ mentions them in this same fashion when He ﷾ talks of the vastness of His blessing on the community in which He ﷾ sent the Messenger, and His great generosity to them, saying: *"Allah did confer a great favour on the believers when He sent among them a Messenger from among themselves, rehearsing unto them the Signs of*

Allah, purifying them, and instructing them in Scripture and Wisdom, even though before that, they had been in manifest error." (3: 164)

He ﷻ also mentions these goals and benefits collectively in *Sūrah* al-Jumu'ah, where He ﷻ talks of the Arabs who were first to have the good fortune of this Prophetic mission, and amongst whom its blessed and pleasing effects appeared; how they were followed then by the non-Arabs so that the whole world experienced this good fortune; and how this mission will remain through the ages *"A goodly tree, whose root is firmly fixed, and its branches (reach) to the heavens. It brings forth its fruit at all times, by the leave of its Lord."* (14: 24–25) This noble verse encompasses the beginning of this blessing, its expansion and spread, and its transmission from one land to another, one generation to another, and one age to another. It mentions the everlasting and abiding nature of the blessing in that the bounty of Allah ﷻ has no end and no limitation. Every age and every generation receives its share of it, *"A gift without end"*. (11: 108) With this addition and expression of favour, these verses complete the previous ones in His saying: *"It is He Who has sent amongst the Unlettered a messenger from among themselves, to rehearse to them His Signs, to purify them, and to instruct them in Scripture and Wisdom – although they had been, before, in manifest error; as well as (to confer all these benefits upon) others of them, who have not already joined them. And He is exalted in Might, Wise. Such is the Bounty of Allah, which He bestows on whom He will, and Allah is the Lord of the highest bounty."* (62: 2–4)

Thus the recitation and teaching of the Book, the teaching of wisdom and the purification of the heart are among the primary goals of the mission. They are the four pillars of the Call to Allah ﷻ and the way in which the reforming and educative miracle of this Prophethood is most completely expressed. Everything else besides this, in terms of legal codification and legislation, legal rulings and details of law, and governance and fighting in the path of Allah ﷻ, are consequences and results of these goals, inherent in them and fulfilling them. So it is clear that the task of refining behaviour and purifying the heart occupies a significant position in the sphere of the Prophetic call and is among the main objectives of the mission of Muḥammad (ﷺ). The Qur'ān indicates that good character and the good manners of Islam are among the most important ways in which wisdom manifests itself. Indeed the Qur'ān often uses the term "wisdom" for these good traits of character and manners.

In *Sūrah* al-Isrā', Allah ﷻ mentions His fundamental ethical teachings in His words, *"Thy Lord hath decreed that ye worship none but Him, and that ye be kind to parents. Whether one or both of them attain old age in thy life, say not to them a word of contempt, nor repel them, but address them in terms of honour. And, out of kindness, lower to them the wing of humility, and say: 'My Lord! bestow on them Thy Mercy even as they cherished me in childhood.' Your Lord knoweth best what is in your hearts: if ye do deeds of righteousness, verily He is Most Forgiving to those who turn to Him again and again (in true penitence). And render to the kindred their due rights, as (also) to those in want, and to the wayfarer: But squander not (your wealth) in the manner of a spendthrift. Verily spendthrifts are brothers of Satans. And Satan is to his Lord (Himself) ungrateful. And even if thou hast to turn away from them in pursuit of the Mercy from thy Lord which thou dost expect, yet speak to them a word of easy kindness. Make not thy hand tied (like a niggard's) to thy neck, nor stretch it forth to its utmost reach, so that thou become blameworthy and destitute. Verily thy Lord doth provide sustenance in abundance for whom He pleaseth, and straiten it; for He doth know and regard all His servants. Kill not your children for fear of want: We shall provide sustenance for them as well as for you: verily the killing of them is a great sin. Nor come nigh to adultery: for it is an indecent (deed) and an evil way. Nor take life – which Allah has made sacred – except for just cause. And if anyone is slain wrongfully, We have given his heir authority (to demand Qiṣāṣ or to forgive): but let him not exceed bounds in the matter of taking life, for he is helped (by the Law). Come not nigh to the orphan's property except to improve it, until he attains the age of full strength, and fulfil (every) engagement, for every engagement will be enquired into (on the Day of Reckoning). Give full measure when ye measure, and weigh with a balance that is straight: that is better and fairer in the final determination. And pursue not that of which thou hast no knowledge; for surely the hearing, the sight, the heart, all of those shall be questioned about that. Nor walk on the earth with insolence: for thou canst not rend the earth asunder, nor reach the mountains in height. Of all such things the evil is hateful in the sight of thy Lord."* (17: 23–38)

These sixteen verses contain the prohibition of *shirk*; the command to be good to parents and behave humbly towards them, and to give to relatives, the poor and travellers, and speak kindly to them; the prohibition of squandering wealth, of excessive generosity or meanness, of killing children, of fornication, of killing anyone without a legal right, of exceeding the limits in retaliation, and of consuming an orphan's property except by legal right; the command to fulfil contracts, and to give full weight and measure; and the prohibition of arrogance and insolence. After concluding these ethical teachings, which form a common ground on which all religions and communities meet, as do the natural upright disposition of humanity, and all sound intellects, Allah ﷻ completes them with His words, *"These are among the (precepts of) wisdom, which thy Lord has revealed to thee."* (17: 39)

That is also the way of the Qur'ān in *Sūrah* Luqmān, except that in *Sūrah* al-Isrā' the mention of wisdom comes at the end of the subject, while in *Sūrah* Luqmān it comes at the beginning. Before talking of Luqmān's ethical teachings, in terms of the prohibition of *shirk*; recognition of the honour accorded to parents, and obedience to them in what is acceptable; following the path of those who have turned wholly to Allah; fear of Allah ﷻ in every matter, whether small or large; establishing prayer; enjoining good and forbidding evil; patience in the face of misfortune; not looking down on people, nor being conceited and arrogant; the instruction to adopt a middle course in all matters – to be moderate in pace when walking and not to raise the voice (all of which can be found in His words from *"Behold, Luqmān said to his son by way of instruction: 'O my son! Join not in worship (others) with Allah: for false worship is indeed the highest wrong-doing.'"* up to *"And be moderate in thy pace, and lower thy voice; for the harshest of sounds without doubt is the braying of the ass."* (31: 13–19)) – before talking of that, Allah opens the subject by saying, *"We bestowed wisdom on Luqmān: 'Show (thy) gratitude to Allah.' And whoever is grateful does so to the profit of his own soul: but if any is ungrateful, verily Allah is free of all wants, worthy of all praise.*" (31: 12) Thus He ﷻ indicates that everything that Luqmān uttered, and the ethical instruction and wise counsel that emerged from him, flowed solely from this wisdom with which Allah ﷻ had honoured Luqmān, and with which He ﷻ singled him out from among his contemporaries: its merit derived from this divine gift and the outstanding moral behaviour that was his natural disposition, and which he took on and was given success in maintaining. For that reason, in the text of this verse, after mentioning the bestowal of this wisdom, He ﷻ says, "*'Show (thy) gratitude to Allah.' And whoever is grateful does so to the profit of his own soul: but if any is ungrateful, verily Allah is free of all wants, worthy of all praise.*"

Thus the word "wisdom" appears in the course of discussing good character and pleasing and noble qualities, such as: spending one's wealth in the way of Allah ﷻ, then not following it up with reminders of one's generosity or words and actions that injure (those who receive the charity); the exhortation to speak kindly and forgive, and to beware of hypocrisy (in performing good actions only for the sake of being seen to do so) and of disbelief in Allah ﷻ; the fear of charity being in vain and good deeds being brought to nothing (by wrong intention or disbelief); putting the self right and keeping it thus; giving from the best of one's wealth and not singling out the worst of it (to be given in charity); the prohibition of excessive fear of poverty and of abandoning oneself to Satan. For example, read the words of Allah ﷻ Most High from *"The parable of those who spend their substance in the way of Allah"* until *"The Evil One threatens you with poverty and bids you to conduct unseemly. Allah promiseth you His forgiveness and bounties. And Allah careth for all and He knoweth all things."* (2: 261–268), all of which He ﷻ concludes with the words, *"He granteth wisdom to whom He pleaseth; and he to whom wisdom is granted receiveth indeed a benefit overflowing; but none will grasp the Message but men of understanding."* (2: 269)

All of this shows that, in the usage of the Qur'ān, wisdom has a profound and unbreakable connection to good character. If there is no good character there is no wisdom. If there is no wisdom there is no good character. Once that is established, then the teaching of good character, the disciplining of the lower self, and the purification of the heart (none of which is complete without the correcting of beliefs, purification from the impurities of *shirk* and ignorance, and taking on sound knowledge) are seen to occupy a significant position in the task of prophethood, and form an important goal among the principal aims of the prophetic mission, and all fall under the heading of teaching wisdom, and purification.

The Prophet ﷺ mentioned this sublime objective of his mission in a single definitive phrase, when he said: "I was only sent to perfect good character." (*Muwaṭṭā'*) At the same time he was the most perfect example of this objective and the best model to be followed to achieve it. The Qur'ān says, *"And thou (standest) on an exalted standard of character."* (68: 4), and when 'Ā'ishah ﵂ was asked about the character of the Prophet ﷺ she said, "His character was the Qur'ān." (Muslim) That is why Allah calls on mankind to follow him and to take him as a perfect and enduring model, when He ﷻ says: *"Ye have indeed in the Messenger of Allah a beautiful pattern (of conduct) for any one whose hope is in Allah and the Final Day, and who engages much in the remembrance of Allah,"* (33: 21) and He ﷻ says, *"Say: 'If ye do love Allah, follow me: Allah will love you and forgive you your sins. For Allah is Oft-Forgiving, Most Merciful.'"* (3: 31)

This wisdom and purification were among the greatest fruits of being in the company of the Prophet ﷺ. So under his care a generation grew up who were adorned with the best possible and noblest qualities of character and who were free of base characteristics, destructive habits, blameworthy qualities, destructive aspects of the self, remnants of the days of ignorance, and the deceptions of Satan. The Qur'ān testifies to the uprightness of their hearts, their righteousness, and their achieving the pinnacle of refinement of character and purification of the self. It says: *"And know that among you is Allah's Messenger. Were he, in many matters, to follow your (wishes), ye would certainly fall into misfortune. But Allah has endeared the Faith to you, and has made it beautiful in your hearts, and He has made hateful to you unbelief, wickedness, and rebellion. Such indeed are those who walk in righteousness – a grace and favour from Allah, and Allah is full of Knowledge and Wisdom."* (49: 7–8)

The Messenger of Allah ﷺ testified on their behalf when he said, "The best of mankind are my generation." (Bukhārī), and in another narration, "The best of my community is my generation." (Bukhārī) One of their companions ('Abdullāh ibn Mas'ūd ﷺ) testified on their behalf with a succinct far-reaching statement when he said of them that they were "the people with the most pious hearts and the deepest knowledge, and they were the least in affectation." One of their enemies even testified for them by saying, "They are horsemen by day and monks by night. They only take food from those under their protection if they pay for it and they only enter with peace. They follow those they fight until they catch up with them." Another said, "They stand in prayer by night and fast by day. They fulfil their covenants and enjoin the right and forbid the wrong and insist on justice from one another."

History resounds with reports of their noble character and virtuous actions, and there are countless stories about their good habits and noble qualities, their intense fear of Allah ﷻ, their making do with little of this world, their preferring the Next World over this world, their preferring others to themselves even when they had more right, their conveying trusts to their owners, their testifying to the truth even to their own detriment, or that of their parents or their relatives, their establishing other's rights as opposed to their own, their supporting the Truth, their anger for the sake of Allah ﷻ and His Messenger ﷺ, their love and hate for the sake of Allah ﷻ, their mercy for all created beings and for the weak, their willingness to share what they had and the high degree to which they established equality of rights, their adherence to truth and justice in every situation, their moderation and temperateness in everything, and so many other noble traits and beautiful qualities which it is unusual to find concentrated in one individual or even one generation.

All these things have been conveyed to us by multiple paths of transmission and are conceded to be true by both Muslims and non-Muslims and all of them derive directly from the teaching of the Prophet ﷺ and the purification extolled by the Qur'ān and mentioned frequently as one of the objectives and benefits of the prophetic mission. The Companions, may Allah be pleased with them all, are nothing more than the ripe crop of Islam, the planted seedlings of prophethood, the products of the prophetic teaching and of the Muḥammadan purification process. And their reality is expressed in the popular verses:

Handicrafts whose craftsman excelled, so they too excelled
And seedlings whose planter was pleasing so they became pleasing too
We were like arrows when they hit their targets,
So too had the archer who let them fly.

When this companionship ended and the Messenger ﷺ joined the Highest Companion ﷻ – as is the inevitable custom of Allah ﷻ with His creation – the recorded words of the Prophet took the place of his company, if anything could possibly take his place, and filled the void which opened up in the life of the Muslims, taking up, in as far as such a thing is possible, the task of refinement and instruction he had undertaken while he was alive. That was the most important subject, and the greatest aim and mission of this elevated science, knowledge of the recorded words and deeds of the Prophet ﷺ. With this knowledge, those who engaged in it renewed their belief, revived their hearts, and purified their souls, putting straight what was crooked in them, rectifying what was corrupt, and healing what was sick. This science was in itself religious knowledge and prophetic medicine. It was *fiqh* and "wisdom". It was the master and teacher, the educator and instructor all at the same time, in addition to which they needed no other knowledge to cultivate their intellects, to rectify their moral character, to gain understanding of the *dīn,* and to reach the highest ranks of *iḥsān* and certainty.

However, over the passage of time, due to the effect of natural, social and legislative factors, the knowledge of *ḥadīth* began to be confined to the science of *aḥkam* (legal rulings). Also the *aḥādīth* form one of the bases of Islamic Jurisprudence (*uṣūl al-fiqh*) and one of the main sources of Islamic law, and Islamic society had naturally and understandably turned its attention to the elaboration of detail in jurisprudence and to the deduction of judicial principles, both out of necessity and because of the emergence of disagreements between the opinions of the *Fuqahā',* and the appearance of schools of Islamic Jurisprudence. As a result, the legalistic and argumentative aspects gained ascendancy over the educational and moral factors in recording the *ḥadīth,* in its teaching and commentary, and in all related fields. Moreover, these aspects became the overwhelming concern of *ḥadīth* scholars, the theme closest to the hearts of its teachers and authors, and their watchword, around which their study revolved, in which they vied for glory and competed with one another, and for the sake of which they expended all their efforts. Indeed, that too was a natural and understandable development dictated by the nature of their situation, differing times, and the logic of necessity. This is why many of those who sought the levels of *iḥsān* (excellence) and *yaqīn* (certainty), and were concerned with the refinement of their character and the purification of their souls sought refuge in a different knowledge (such as *taṣawwuf*) and with different men in order to quench their thirst, to fill their hearts, and to satisfy a need in their souls.

However, many great *ḥadīth* scholars felt the need of all Muslims, and particularly the seekers of knowledge of the *dīn* and its inner reality, for a reliable collection of *aḥādīth* of the Prophet ﷺ whose subject matter was confined to the refinement of moral character, the purification of the heart, the acquisition of virtues and elimination of vices, the attainment of the levels of *iḥsān* and *yaqīn*, and entry into the ranks of the absolutely sincere and truthful. To this end, they wrote books both small and large, both famous and unknown. Three among them are well-known and achieved considerable acceptance, and the scholars of this discipline, both ancient and modern, have devoted their attention to them. One of them is the book *al-Adab al-Mufrad*, by the accepted leader in the field of *ḥadīth,* Imām Muḥammad ibn Ismā'īl al-Bukhārī (194–256 AH), the author of the famous *Ṣaḥīḥ* Collection *al-Jāmi' aṣ-Ṣaḥīḥ*. The second is the book *at-Targhīb wa't-Tarhīb*, by the great Ḥāfiẓ Zakiyyu'd-dīn 'Abdu'l-'Aẓīm ibn 'Abdi'l-Qawī, Abū Muḥammad al-Mundhirī ad-Dimashqī (581–656 AH). The third is the *Riyāḍ aṣ-Ṣāliḥīn min Kalāmi Sayyid al-Mursalīn*, by Imām Abū Zakariyyā Muḥyiddīn Yaḥyā an-

Nawawī (631–676 AH), the author of the commentary on the *Ṣaḥīḥ* of Muslim, and of other great books about *ḥadīth* and the men who transmitted them.

Al-Adab al-Mufrad, as its name indicates, deals with behaviour and morals. It has not obtained the renown and attention befitting the illustriousness of its author and has not been selected as teaching material. It has not been accorded the appropriate level of concern, to such an extent that it was not made available in printed form till relatively recently.

At-Targhīb wa't-Tarhīb by al-Mundhirī, is a large and compendious collection which, despite its illustriousness, is not useful in the initial stages of study of the noble *ḥadīth*. It contains every type of *ḥadīth*, its author, may Allah ﷻ give him an ample reward, having not confined himself only to sound and accepted *ḥadīth* or to the *aḥādīth* of the six authentic collections.

As for the *Riyāḍ aṣ-Ṣāliḥīn*, though it has begun to be accepted, like most of the books of Imām an-Nawawī, the interest shown in it is of comparatively recent origin. It has now been republished several times and made part of the curriculum in many religious schools, and most people active in the sphere of *da'wah,* reform, and education give it their attention. It has lately become very widespread but it is quite large and of a high standard in relation to the capacities of most young students in religious schools.[1]

In the light of this, many educators and people dealing with the correct upbringing of young people in general, and of those studying in religious schools in particular, have become aware of the need for a small book, not burdensome, and written in a simple style, in which the author confines himself to the important questions of behaviour and extracts from the great treasury of the Qur'ān, *Sunnah* and the collections of *ḥadīth* whatever is needed most, can easily be acted upon, and is most universal in benefit. It should provide a sound

1. We are grateful to Allah, the Exalted, that we have been able to translate the above-mentioned three books. As for *at-Targhīb wa't-Tarhīb*, we used the version abridged by Imām Ḥāfiẓ ibn Ḥajar, may Allah have mercy on him, which was edited and published by Maulānā Ḥabīb-ur-Raḥmān A'ẓamī (d. 1992), who is regarded as one of the greatest scholars of the sciences of *Ḥadīth* and Asmā' ar-Rijāl (biographies of the transmitters of *ḥadīth*) – Iqbāl Aḥmad A'ẓamī.

foundation and be an illuminating lamp for young students. It should act as a guide for them in their lives and encourage them to obedience and good actions, and warn them against depravity and blameworthy characteristics. It should help them to prepare their hearts and their understanding for the approach to this pure source and partaking of its abundant waters. It should also serve as an introduction to the books which they will study later in this field.

Because of my close relationship with him and my preoccupation with his scholarly works, I knew that my father, Maulānā 'Abdu'l-Ḥayy al-Ḥasanī, had composed a small book on this subject entitled *Talkhīṣ al-Akhbār*, for which he had written a commentary spanning several notebooks, entitled *Muntaha'l-Afkār fī Sharḥ Talkhīṣ al-Akhbār*. I knew of his immense love for the *ḥadīth* of the Prophet (ﷺ), his unsparing efforts to obtain them from the Imāms of this science, his distinction among his contemporaries in this science, and his high rank in it. However, I was engaged in publishing his books about history and biographies, like *Nuzhatu'l-Khawāṭir*, *ath-Thaqāfah al-Islāmiyyah fi'l-Hind*, and *al-Hind fi'l-'Ahd al-Islāmī* and this distracted me from paying attention to this book and making it available to people.

When I perceived the desire of some educators and patrons of religious schools for an intermediate book on this subject which would be easy to teach, I became interested in this book of my father and dug it out from among his books and manuscripts. I read it with careful attention and consideration and found it to be a valuable book, in spite of its small size, in which the author had confined himself to sound *aḥādīth* from the six authentic collections, predominantly from the collections of al-Bukhārī and Muslim. It shows the excellence of the author's choice, as is the case in all his books, the soundness of his taste, his open-mindedness in selection of *ḥadīth* and in giving preference to some *ḥadīth* over others, and his avoidance of being partisan. He was familiar with the spirit of the age, and directly aware of the abilities of students in the religious institutes because for a time he taught in the *Dār al-'Ulūm* of the *Nadwatu'l-'Ulamā'* (Council of Religious Scholars), and he also spent a period as director of the *Nadwatu'l-'Ulamā'* and supervisor of education in the *Dār al-'Ulūm* connected to it.

He added useful comments to the book in his own hand, being concerned with the explanation of unusual words, making the meaning of the *aḥādīth* clear, and clarifying their aims where such clarification was necessary. In this way the book came to be complete in itself, achieving the required aim, conforming with both the spirit of the age and the level of scholarship of the initial stages of education.

That is why my determination to publish this religious and educational work is sound, for it fulfils the urgent need of the religious schools and facilitates the spread of the *ḥadīth,* as well as being a kindness to my father and going some way towards fulfilling the duty I owe him. Hopefully by publishing the book and adding it to those already published on this subject, I will share in the reward for directing the teaching of the *aḥādīth* of the Prophet ﷺ towards the aim which was one of the most important goals of the prophetic mission: namely the purification of the heart, the refinement of moral character, and the struggle to reach the rank of *iḥsān,* and for according that aim its due importance in the *dīn.* We ask Allah ﷻ to benefit by it all those seeking knowledge of the *dīn* and indeed all Muslims, and to make it a treasury of good for its author, and a means to righteous action for all who strive on its behalf and devote their effort to it.

May Allah ﷻ bless the best of His creation, our leader and master Muḥammad, and his family and all his Companions, and grant them peace.

Abu'l-Ḥasan 'Alī al-Ḥasanī an-Nadwī

بسم الله الرحمن الرحيم

In the name of Allah, the Merciful, the Compassionate,
and to Him alone we pray for help

AUTHOR'S PREFACE

Praise belongs to Allah, the Lord of the worlds. The good outcome is for the Godfearing. There is no aggression except against wrongdoers. I testify that there is no god but Allah alone with no partner, the Lord of the universe and the God of the Messengers. I testify that our master Muḥammad ﷺ is His slave and Messenger, who was sent as a mercy to the worlds, as a path for travellers, and as proof against all who are legally obligated (to observe the precepts of Islam). May Allah bless him and his noble family and pure Companions throughout time, and grant them abundant peace.

'Abdu'l-Ḥayy ibn Fakhru'd-Dīn ibn 'Abdu'l-'Alī, totally dependent on Allah, the Truly Independent, says: This is a summary of reports related from the Prophet ﷺ who was protected from error. I have chosen them from sound *aḥādīth* which deal with refinement of character, purification of the heart, and the cleansing of the outward and inward, in the hope that Allah will benefit me through it on the Day of Repayment, that it will encourage those who read it to perform good deeds, and that it will guide to the path of salvation in this life and after death. We seek refuge in Allah, the All-Glorious, from knowledge which does not benefit, a heart which is not humble, a self whose appetites are never satisfied, and a supplication which is not accepted. He is sufficient unto me and the best Guardian, the best Protector and the best Helper.

Sayyed 'Abdu'l-Ḥayy al-Ḥasanī

I

TAWḤĪD

Allah, Exalted is He, says: *"And your God is One God: There is no god but He, Most Gracious, Most Merciful."* (2: 163)

He ﷻ says: *"Allah! There is no god but He — the Living, the Self-subsisting, Eternal. No slumber can seize Him nor sleep."* (2: 255)

He ﷻ says: *"Allah (Himself) is witness that there is no god but He, as are His angels, and those endued with knowledge, standing firm on justice. There is no god but He, the Exalted in Power, the Wise."* (3: 18)

He ﷻ says: *"Say: 'O People of the Book! Come to common terms as between us and you: that we worship none but Allah; that we associate no partners with Him; that we erect not, from among ourselves, lords and patrons other than Allah.' If then they turn back, say ye: 'Bear witness that we are Muslims (bowing to Allah's will.)"* (3: 64)

He ﷻ says: *"It is not (possible) that a man, to whom is given the Book, and Wisdom, and the Prophetic Office, should say to people: 'Be ye my worshippers rather than Allah's.' On the contrary, (he would say): 'Be ye worshippers of Him Who is truly the Cherisher of all: for ye have taught the Book and ye have studied it earnestly.'"* (3: 79)

He ﷻ says: *"With Him are the keys of the Unseen, the treasures that none knoweth but He. He knoweth whatever there is on the earth and in the sea. Not a leaf doth fall but with His knowledge: there is not a grain in the darkness (or depths) of the earth, nor anything fresh or dry (green or withered), but is (inscribed) in a Record Clear."* (6: 59)

He ﷻ says: *"He is the Originator of the heavens and the earth: How can He have a son when He hath no consort? He created all things, and He hath full knowledge of all things. That is Allah, your Lord! There is no god but He, the Creator of all things; then worship ye Him; and He hath power to dispose of all affairs.*" (6: 101–102)

He ﷻ says: "*Allah is He, than Whom there is no other god – Who knows (all things) both secret and open; He is the Most Gracious, the Most Merciful. Allah is He, than Whom there is no other god – The Sovereign, the Holy One, the Source of Peace (and Perfection), the Guardian of Faith, the Preserver of Safety, the Exalted in Might, the Irresistible, the Supreme: Glory to Allah! (High is He) above the partners they attribute to Him. He is Allah, the Creator, the Evolver, the Bestower of Forms (or colours). To Him belong the Most Beautiful Names. Whatever is in the heavens and the earth doth declare His praises and glory; and He is the exalted in Might, the Wise.*" (59: 22–24)

He ﷻ says: "*Allah! There is no god but He – the Living, the Self-subsisting, Eternal. No slumber can seize Him nor sleep. His are all things in the heavens and on earth. Who is there can intercede in His presence except as He permitteth? He knoweth what (appeareth to His creatures as) before or after or behind them. Nor shall they compass aught of His knowledge except as He willeth.*" (2: 255)

He ﷻ says: "*Say: 'He is Allah, the One and Only; Allah, the Eternal, Absolute. He begetteth not nor is He begotten, and there is none like unto Him.'*" (112: 1–4)

He ﷻ says: "*Verily the knowledge of the Hour is with Allah (alone). It is He Who sends down rain, and He Who knows what is in the wombs. No one knows what it is that he will earn tomorrow; nor does anyone know in what land he is to die.*" (31: 34)

He ﷻ says, relating from Yūsuf: "*O my two companions of the prison! (I ask you): are many lords differing among themselves better, or Allah, the One, Supreme and Irresistible? If not Him, ye worship nothing but names which ye have named – ye and your fathers – for which Allah hath sent down no authority: the Command is for none but Allah. He hath commanded that ye worship none but Him. That is the right religion, but most men understand not.*" (12: 39–40)

He 🌸 says: *"Say: 'I am but a man like yourselves, (but) the inspiration has come to me, that your God is One God. Whoever expects to meet his Lord, let him work righteousness, and in the worship of his Lord admit no one as partner."* (18: 110)

1. It is reported from 'Abdullāh b. 'Abbās 🌸 that when the Messenger of Allah 🌸 sent Mu'ādh ibn Jabal to the people of Yemen he said, "You are going to a nation who are among the People of the Book. The first thing you call them to should be the recognition of Allah's oneness. When they acknowledge that, then tell them that Allah has made the five prayers obligatory on them daily." (Bukhārī)

2. It is reported that Mu'ādh ibn Jabal 🌸 said that the Prophet 🌸 said, "O Mu'ādh! Do you know what is Allah's right on His slaves?" He said, "Allah and His Messenger know best." He said, "That they worship Him and not associate anything with Him. Do you know what is their right on Him?" He said, "Allah and His Messenger know best. " He said, "That He does not punish them." (Bukhārī)

3. It is reported from 'Abdullāh Ibn 'Umar 🌸 that the Prophet 🌸 said, "The keys to the Unseen are five things which only Allah knows: no one knows what is inside the wombs except Allah; no one knows what will happen tomorrow except Allah; no one knows when the rain will come except Allah; no soul knows what land it will die in except Allah; and no one knows when the Last Hour will come except Allah." (Bukhārī)

4. It is reported that Zayd b. Khālid al-Juhanī 🌸 said, "The Messenger of Allah 🌸 led us in the morning prayer at Ḥudaybiyyah after rain had fallen in the night. When he finished, he faced the people and said, 'Do you know what your Lord has said?' They said, 'Allah and His Messenger know best.' He said, 'He said, "Some of my slaves have reached the morning believing in Me and some disbelieving. As for the one who said, 'It rained upon us by the bounty of Allah', he is the one who believes in Me and disbelieves in the stars; and as for the one who said, 'It rained upon

us through (the setting of) such-and-such a star,' he is the one who disbelieves in Me and believes in the stars." ' " (Muslim)

5. It is reported that Mu'āwiyah ibn al-Ḥakam said, "I said, 'Messenger of Allah, I am newly come from *Jāhiliyyah*. Allah has brought us Islam but some men among us still go to the soothsayers.' 'He said, "Do not go to them." ' I said, 'Some men among us still look for bad omens.' He said, 'That is something which they find in their hearts, but they should not let it deter them.' I said, 'Some men among us draw lines (to predict the future).' He said, 'One of the Prophets used to draw such lines. If someone's drawing lines corresponds to what he (that Prophet) used to do, that is all right.' " (Muslim)

6. It is reported from Abū Hurayrah that the Messenger of Allah said, "There is no automatic contagion,[1] no bad omens, no avenging spirit,[2] and no serpent biting the hungry belly."[3] (Bukhārī)

7. It is reported that Ibn 'Abbās said, "One day I was (riding) behind the Prophet and he said, 'Young lad, I will teach you some words. Bear Allah in mind and He will bear you in mind. Bear Allah in mind and you will find Him before you. When you ask, ask Allah. When you seek help, seek Allah's help. Know that if the whole community of Muslims were to agree to help you in some way, they could not help you in any way except what Allah Most High has decreed for you. And if the whole community were to agree to harm you in some way, they could not harm you in any way except what Allah has decreed for you. The pens have been lifted and the pages are dry.' "[4] (Tirmidhī)

1. That is, catching a disease only happens by the will of Allah, not because of being close to somebody with that disease.

2. *Hāmah*: a superstitious belief of the pre-Islamic Arabs, that the unavenged spirit of a murdered person took the form of a night bird.

3. Another pre-Islamic superstition.

4. What will happen has already been decreed and nothing will change that.

8. It is reported that Anas said that the Messenger of Allah said, "Let each of you ask his Lord for all his needs, to the extent that he even asks Him for a sandal-strap when it is broken." (Tirmidhī)

9. It is related that 'Adī ibn Ḥātim said, "I went to the Prophet with a gold cross on my neck. He said, 'O 'Adī! Throw away this idol.' I heard him recite from *Sūrah* Barā'ah [al-Tawbah], *'They take their priests and their anchorites to be their lords in derogation of Allah.'* (9: 31) He said, 'They did not actually worship them, but when they made something lawful for them, they also considered it lawful, and when they made something unlawful for them, they considered it unlawful." (Tirmidhī)

10. It is reported that Qays ibn Sa'd ibn 'Ubādah al-Anṣārī said, "I went to al-Ḥīrah and saw them prostrating to one of their leaders. I said to myself, 'It would be more fitting for the people to prostrate to the Messenger of Allah.' So when I came to the Messenger of Allah I told him, 'I went to al-Ḥīrah and saw the people prostrating to one of their leaders, yet you have more right to be prostrated to.' He said to me, 'Do you think that if you were to pass by my grave, you would prostrate to it?' I said, 'No.' He said, 'Then do not do that.' " (Abū Dāwūd)

11. It is reported that Jubayr ibn Muṭ'im said, "A bedouin came to the Messenger of Allah and said, 'People are struggling, families are starving, wealth has been exhausted, and the livestock has perished. Ask Allah to give us rain! We ask you to intercede with Allah on our behalf and we ask Allah to intercede with you on our behalf.' The Prophet said, 'Glory be to Allah! Glory be to Allah!' He continued to say that until unease about it was visible in the faces of his Companions. Then he said, 'Woe to you! It is not possible to ask Allah to intercede with any of His creation. Allah's situation is far beyond that!' " (Abū Dāwūd)

12. It is reported that ar-Rubayyi' bint Mu'awwidh ibn 'Afrā' said, "The Prophet came in after my marriage had been consummated

and sat on my bed just like you are sitting now, and our girls started beating the tambourines and reciting verses about the elder men of my family who had been martyred at Badr. Then one of them said, 'Among us is a Prophet who knows what will happen tomorrow.' And he said, 'Leave this and recite what you were reciting before.' " (Bukhārī)

13. It is reported from Ibn 'Abbās ؓ that 'Umar ؓ said: The Messenger of Allah ﷺ said, "Do not go to excess in praising me as the Christians went to excess about 'Isa ibn Maryam, peace be upon him. I am His slave, so say, 'His slave and His Messenger.' " (Bukhārī)

14. It is reported that Abū Hurayrah ؓ said that the Messenger of Allah ﷺ said, "None of you should say, ' '*abdī* (my slave)' or '*amatī* (my slave-girl)'. All of you are slaves of Allah. Instead you should say, '*ghulāmī* (my boy), *jāriyatī* (my girl) and *fatāya* (my lad) and *fatātī* (my young lady).' Nor should a slave say, '*rabbī* (my lord)'. Instead he should say, '*sayyidī* (my owner)', or '*mawlāya* (my master)'." One variant has, "Nor should a slave say to his owner, '*mawlāya* (my master)'. Your Master is Allah." (Muslim)

15. It is reported that Ibn 'Umar ؓ said that the Messenger of Allah ﷺ said, "Indeed Allah forbids you to swear by your fathers. Whoever is going to swear, should swear by Allah or be silent." (Bukhārī, Muslim)

16. From 'Ābis b. Rabī'ah who said, "I saw 'Umar ibn al-Khaṭṭāb ؓ kiss the Black Stone, saying, 'I know that you are just a stone which can neither harm nor help. If I had not seen the Messenger of Allah ﷺ kiss you, I would not have kissed you either.' " (Bukhārī, Muslim)

2

SINCERITY IN WORSHIP

Sincerity is to devote oneself in obedience to Allah ﷻ alone.

Allah ﷻ, says: *"And they have been commanded no more than this: to worship Allah, offering Him sincere devotion, being true (in faith); to establish regular prayer; and to practise regular charity; and that is the religion right and straight."* (98: 5)

He ﷻ says: *"It is not their meat nor their blood that reaches Allah. It is your piety that reaches Him."* (22: 37)

He ﷻ says: *"Cancel not your charity by reminders of your generosity or by hurting [others] – like those who spend their substance to be seen of men."* (2: 264)

He ﷻ says: *"They stand without earnestness to be seen of men, but little do they hold Allah in remembrance."* (4: 142)

He ﷻ says: *"Is it not to Allah that sincere devotion is due?"* (39: 3)

17. It is related that 'Abdullāh ibn 'Umar ﵁ said, "I heard the Messenger of Allah ﷺ say: 'Three men of a previous generation were travelling and took refuge for the night in a cave. They entered it and a rock fell down the mountain and blocked the entrance. They said, "The only thing that will rescue us from this rock is to call on Allah invoking good actions we have done!" One of them said, "O Allah, my parents were both old and it was my habit never to give milk in the evening either to my family or servants before giving it to them first. One day I went a long way in search of pasture for my flocks and did not reach them until they had already gone to bed. I milked their evening drink but found them asleep. I

did not want to wake them nor to give my family or servants their evening drink before they had had theirs, so I remained with the cup in my hand waiting for them to wake up until dawn came. The children were at my feet, crying because of hunger. Then they woke up and drank their drink. O Allah, if I did that out of the desire for Your Face, then rescue us from the situation we are in with this rock." The rock opened up a little but they still could not get out. The second said, "O Allah! A girl cousin of mine was the person I loved more than any other. (Another variant has, 'I used to love one of my uncle's daughters with the most intense love it is possible for a man to have for a woman.') I tried to seduce her and she refused me until, one year when she was in dire need, she came to me and I gave her a hundred and twenty *dīnār* provided that she would let me do what I wanted with her. She agreed but when I was about to have my way with her, (one variant has, 'when I was between her legs') she said, 'Fear Allah and do not break the seal without having the right to do so.' Then I left her alone in spite of the fact that she was, of all people, the one I loved the most and also left her with the gold I had given her. O Allah, if I did that out of the desire for Your Face, then rescue us from our situation!" The rock moved a little further but they still could not get out. The third said, "O Allah, I employed some workers and gave all of them their wages except for one man who went off without taking what he was owed. I invested his wage until it multiplied in value. After a time he came to me and said, 'O man, pay me my wage!' I said, 'All the camels, cattle, sheep and slaves that you see here have come from your wage.' He said, 'Man, do not make fun of me?' I said, 'I am not making fun of you.' He took them all and drove them off, not leaving anything. O Allah, if I did that out of the desire for Your Face, then rescue us from the situation we are in!" The rock moved away and they walked out.' " (Bukhārī, Muslim and the wording is of Bukhārī)

18. It is related that Abū Hurayrah ﷺ said, "I heard the Messenger of Allah ﷺ say, 'The first of people to be judged on the Day of Rising will be a man who was martyred. He will be brought and will be informed of the blessings he had and will acknowledge them. Allah will say, "What did you do with them?"

He will say, "I fought for You until I was martyred." Allah will say, "You lie. Rather you fought so it would be said, 'He is a bold man!' And so it was said." Then the command will be given and he will be dragged on his face until he is thrown into the Fire. There will also be a man who acquired knowledge and taught it and recited the Qur'ān. He will be brought forward and informed of his blessings which he will acknowledge. Allah will say, "What did you do with them?" He will say, "I acquired knowledge and taught it and I recited the Qur'ān for Your sake." He will say, "You lie. Rather you studied so that it would be said, 'He is a scholar!' And you recited so that it would be said, 'He is a reciter!' And so it was said." Then the command will be given and he will be dragged on his face until he is thrown into the Fire. There will also be a man to whom Allah gave a lot of wealth and all sorts of property. He will be brought and informed of his blessings which he will acknowledge. Allah will say, "What did you do with them?" He will say, "There was no path in which You like spending to be done but that I spent in it for You." He will say, "You lie. Rather you did it so that it would be said, 'He is generous.' And so it was said." Then the command will be given and he will be dragged on his face until he is thrown into the Fire.' " (Muslim)

19. It is related that Abū Umāmah said, "A man came to the Messenger of Allah and said, 'What do you think about a man who goes on military expeditions seeking material reward and fame?' The Messenger of Allah said, 'He obtains nothing.' He repeated it three times and the Messenger of Allah said, 'He obtains nothing.' Then he said, 'Allah, the Mighty and Exalted, only accepts action that is done sincerely for Him and by which His Countenance is sought." (Abū Dāwūd, an-Nasā'ī)

20. It is related from Anas ibn Mālik that the Messenger of Allah said, "Anyone who leaves this world with sincere devotion for Allah alone, and worshipping Him without partner, establishing the prayer and paying the *zakāt*, will die while Allah is pleased with him." (Ibn Mājah)

21. It is related that Abū Hurayrah ﷺ said that the Messenger of Allah ﷺ said, "Anyone who learns the kind of knowledge which should be used in seeking the Face of Allah, the Majestic and Great, and only learns it in order to obtain some of the goods of this world through it, will not experience the scent of the Garden on the Day of Rising." (Abū Dāwūd)

22. Abū Hurayrah ﷺ said: I heard the Messenger of Allah ﷺ say, "Allah Almighty says, 'I am He who is least in need of a partner. If anyone does an action, making other than Me a partner in it, I leave him to his partner.' " (Muslim)

23. It is related that Abū Hurayrah ﷺ said that the Messenger of Allah ﷺ said, "At the end of time men will emerge who will seek this world through the *dīn*. They will wear sheep-skins for people to give the impression of meekness. Their tongues are sweeter than honey while their hearts are like those of wolves. Allah, the Mighty and Majestic, will say, 'Are they deluding Me or are they insolent against Me? I swear by Myself that I will send on them from among themselves trials which will leave even the forbearing bewildered.' " (Tirmidhī)

24. It is related that Zayd ibn Thābit ﷺ said that the Messenger of Allah ﷺ said, "May Allah have mercy on those who hear my words and convey them to others. If a Muslim's heart possesses three traits it will never be affected by faithlessness, those of acting sincerely for Allah alone, giving good counsel to the leaders of the Muslims, and holding to the community. Their supplication encompasses those coming after them. If anyone has this world as his goal, Allah will afflict him with poverty and disperse his property and only what is written for him will come to him. If anyone has the Next World for his goal, Allah will put wealth in his heart and make his property sufficient for him and this world will come to him in spite of itself." (Aḥmad, Darīmī and Ibn Mājah)

25. It is related that Abū Hurayrah ﷺ said that the Messenger of Allah ﷺ said, "Allah does not look at your bodies or your forms; He looks at your hearts." (Muslim)

26. It is related that 'Umar ibn al-Khaṭṭāb ﷺ said that he heard the Messenger of Allah ﷺ say, "Actions are only according to intentions. And everyone obtains what he intends. Anyone, therefore, who emigrates for the sake of Allah and His Messenger, his emigration is indeed to Allah and His Messenger. But anyone who emigrates to gain something of this world or to marry a woman, his emigration is for that to which he emigrated."[1] (Bukhārī, Muslim)

1. This is one of the major *aḥādīth* around which the *dīn* is based. It is related from *Imām* Shāfi'ī (may Allah have mercy on him) who said that this *ḥadīth* is the base of the third of all knowledge and it enters in seventy subjects of Islamic jurisprudence.

3

CLINGING TO THE QUR'ĀN AND THE *SUNNAH*

Allah, Exalted is He, says, *"Nothing have We neglected in the Book."* (6: 38)

He ﷻ says, *"If ye differ in anything among yourselves, refer it to Allah and the Messenger."* (4: 59)

He ﷻ says, *"But no, by thy Lord, they can have no (real) Faith, until they make thee judge in all disputes between them, and find in their souls no resistance against thy decisions, but accept them with the fullest conviction."* (4: 65)

He ﷻ says, *"The answer of the believers, when summoned to Allah and His Messenger, in order that he may judge between them, is no other than this: They say, 'We hear and we obey.'"* (24: 51)

He ﷻ says, *"So take what the Messenger gives to you, and abstain from that which he forbids you."* (59: 7)

He ﷻ says, *"Say: 'If ye do love Allah, follow me: Allah will love you and forgive you your sins.'"* (3: 31)

He ﷻ says, *"Ye have indeed in the Messenger of Allah a beautiful pattern (of conduct) for any one whose hope is in Allah and the Final Day, and who engages much in the remembrance of Allah."* (33: 21)

He ﷻ says, *"Let those beware who withstand the Messenger's order, lest some trial befall them, or a grievous penalty be inflicted on them."* (24: 63)

27. It is related that Jābir رضي الله عنه said, "When the Messenger of Allah ﷺ gave an address, his eyes would become red, he would raise his

voice and he would become very angry until he was like someone admonishing an army who says, *'sabbaḥakum,* and *massāhkum* (Guard yourselves against attack).' He would say, 'I have been sent at a time when the Last Hour is (near) like these two,' and he joined together his index finger and middle finger. After glorifying Allah he would say, 'The best speech is the Book of Allah. The best guidance is the guidance of Muḥammad ﷺ. The worst of matters are the new ones (fabrications), and every innovation is misguidance.' Then he would say, 'I am closer to every believer than his own self. Whoever leaves property, it is for his family. Whoever leaves a debt or young children who need support, it is to me (to pay it) and on me (to support them).' " (Muslim)

28. It is related that al-'Irbāḍ ibn Sāriyah ﵁ said, "The Messenger of Allah ﷺ gave us a profound exhortation which made our hearts afraid and our eyes weep. We said, 'O Messenger of Allah, it is an exhortation which is as if it were bidding us farewell, so advise us.' He said, 'I commend you to be fearful of Allah and to hear and obey, even if an [Abyssinian] slave is put in command over you. Any among you who live long will see much disagreement, so you must hold to my *Sunnah* and the *Sunnah* of the rightly-guided and guiding Caliphs. Hold onto it with your teeth. Beware of innovated matters. For every new thing in the religion is innovation and every innovation is misguidance.' " (Abū Dāwūd, Tirmidhī)

29. It is related from Abū Mūsā al-Ash'arī ﵁ that the Prophet ﷺ said, "The example of me and that with which Allah has sent me is that of a man who comes to some people and says, 'O people! I have seen with my own eyes an army coming. I am an open warner to you, so save yourselves! Save yourselves!' A group of them obey him and go out stealthily during the night and are safe while another group deny him and so the army captures them in the morning and kills them. That is the example of those who obey me and follow that with which I have been sent and the example of those who disobey me and deny the truth I have brought." (Bukhārī)

30. It is related that 'Ubādah ibn aṣ-Ṣāmit said, "We gave the Messenger of Allah our pledge to hear and obey in hardship and ease, with regard to both what we liked and what we disliked, even if there was prejudice against us; and not to dispute the authority of those placed over us unless they were proven guilty of clear disbelief in Allah Almighty; and to speak the truth wherever we were and not to fear in the way of Allah the blame of any critic." (Bukhārī, Muslim)

31. It is related that 'Ā'ishah said, "The Prophet did something deliberately setting an easy example for other people, but some people refrained from doing it. When the Prophet learned of that, he delivered a sermon, and after having praised Allah, he said, 'What is wrong with certain people who refrain from doing something that I do? By Allah, I know Allah better than they do, and I am more afraid of Him than they are.' " (Bukhārī)

32. It is related that 'Abdullāh ibn 'Amr ibn al-'Āṣ said, "I heard the Prophet say, 'Allah will not remove knowledge after He has given it to you, but it will be removed when the people of knowledge die and ignorant people remain who will be asked to give *fatawā* (legal ruling) and will give them according to their own opinions. They will go astray and lead others astray.' " (Bukhārī)

33. It is related that Anas ibn Mālik said that the Messenger of Allah said, "Have nothing to do with anyone who is averse to my *Sunnah*." (Muslim)

34. 'Ā'ishah related that the Messenger of Allah said, "Anyone who introduces an innovation in this affair of ours which is not part of it, it will be rejected." (Bukhārī, Muslim)[1]

---

1. This *ḥadīth* is among the most fundamental teachings of Islam. It is like a scale for the deeds. Just as any deed which is not done exclusively for Allah's pleasure, the person who did it will not have a reward from Allah for it, so the same applies for a deed which has no proof from Allah and His Messenger. It will be thrown back on the doer. Every deed of a man must be sincerely for Allah's sake and must be according to the teachings of Allah and His Messenger.

4

LOVE FOR ALLAH ﷻ AND HIS MESSENGER ﷺ

Allah, Exalted is He, says. *"Say: 'If it be that your fathers, your sons, your brothers, your mates, or your kindred; the wealth that ye have gained, the commerce in which ye fear a decline, or the dwellings in which ye delight – are dearer to you than Allah, or His Messenger, or the striving in His cause, then wait until Allah brings about His Decision.' "* (9: 24)

He ﷻ says, *"O ye who believe! If any from among you turn back from his Faith, soon will Allah produce a people whom He will love as they will love Him."* (5: 54)

He ﷻ says, *"But those of faith are overflowing in their love for Allah."* (2: 165)

35. It is related from Anas ibn Mālik ؓ that the Messenger of Allah ﷺ said, "Whoever possesses three attributes will experience the sweetness of belief: that he loves Allah and His Messenger more than anything else; that he loves someone for the sake of Allah alone; and that he would hate to revert to disbelief as much as he would hate to be thrown into the fire." (Bukhārī, Muslim)

36. From Anas ibn Mālik, ؓ who said, "The Messenger of Allah ﷺ said, 'None of you will believe until he loves me more than his parents, children and all the people.' " (Bukhārī)

37. It is related from Anas ibn Mālik ؓ that the Messenger of Allah said, "None of you will believe until he loves me more than his family, his property and all people." (Muslim)

38. Anas ibn Mālik ﷺ also said, "A bedouin said to the Messenger of Allah ﷺ, 'When will the Hour come?' The Messenger of Allah ﷺ said, 'What have you prepared for it?' He said, 'The love of Allah and His Messenger.' He said, 'You will be with the one you love.' " Anas ﷺ said, "I love Allah and His Messenger and (I love) Abū Bakr and 'Umar ﷺ and I hope to be with them, even if I have not done what they have done." (Muslim)

39. It is related that 'Abdullāh ibn 'Umar ﷺ said, "A man came to the Messenger of Allah ﷺ and said, 'O Messenger of Allah, what do you say about a man who loves some people but does not catch up with them (to do as they do)?' The Messenger of Allah ﷺ said, 'A man is with the one he loves.' " (Muslim)

40. It is related from Abū Hurayrah ﷺ that the Messenger of Allah ﷺ said, "Allah Almighty said, 'I declare war against anyone who shows hostility towards a friend of Mine. The most beloved thing with which My slave comes near to Me is what I have made obligatory for him; and My slave keeps on coming closer to Me through supererogatory actions until I love him. When I love him, I become his hearing with which he hears, his sight with which he sees, his hand with which he grips and his foot with which he walks. If he asks Me, I will give to him; and if he asks for My protection, I will protect him.' " (Bukhārī)

5

LOVE FOR THE FAMILY OF
THE PROPHET ﷺ

Allah, Exalted is He, says, *"And Allah only wishes to remove all abomination from you, ye members of the Family, and to make you pure and spotless."* (33: 33)

He ﷻ says, *"Say: 'No reward do I ask of you for this except the love of those near of kin.'"* (42: 23)

He ﷻ says, *"Whoever holds in honour the symbols of Allah (in the sacrifice of animals), such (honour) should come truly from piety of heart."* (22: 32)

41. It is related that Zayd b. Arqam ؓ said, "The Messenger of Allah ﷺ stood up among us one day to address us at a watering-place called Khum between Makkah and Madīnah. He praised and glorified Allah, admonished and reminded people and then said, 'O people! I am a mortal and the messenger of my Lord will soon come to me and I will respond. I leave you two great things. The first is the Book of Allah which contains guidance and light. So take the Book of Allah and cling firmly to it.' He promoted the Book of Allah and stimulated our desire for it. Then he said, 'And the people of my house. I remind you of Allah with respect to the people of my house. I remind you of Allah with respect to the people of my house.' " (Muslim)

42. It is related that 'Ā'ishah ؓ said, "The Prophet ﷺ went out one morning wrapping around himself a stripped cloak woven from black (camel) hair and al-Ḥasan ibn 'Alī ؓ came and he drew him

inside it, and then al-Ḥusayn ؊ came and he drew him in and then Fatimah ؊ came and he drew her inside and then ʿAlī ؊ came and he drew him inside it, and then he recited, *'And Allah only wishes to remove all abomination from you, ye members of the Family, and to make you pure and spotless.'* (33: 33)" (Muslim)

43. Al-Miswar b. Makhramah ؊ related that the Messenger of Allah ﷺ said, "Fatimah is part of me. Whoever makes her angry makes me angry." (Bukhārī)

44. It is related that al-Barāʾ ibn ʿĀzib ؊ said, "I saw the Messenger of Allah ﷺ with al-Ḥasan ibn ʿAlī on his shoulder. He said, 'O Allah, I love him, so love him!' " (Bukhārī)

45. It is related that Anas ibn Mālik ؊ said, "There was no one who resembled the Prophet ﷺ more than al-Ḥasan b. ʿAlī ؊." (Bukhārī)

46. It is related from ʿAbdullāh ibn ʿUmar ؊ that he said: "The people of Iraq asked me for a *fatwā* about the killing of a fly (in the state of *Iḥrām*) while they have killed the son of the Prophet's daughter, and the Prophet ﷺ has said about her children (al-Ḥasan and al-Ḥusain): 'That they are my flowers in this world'."[1] (Bukhārī)

47. It is related that Anas ibn Mālik ؊ said, "The Messenger of Allah ﷺ was asked, 'Which of the people of your house do you love most?' He said, 'Al-Ḥasan and al-Ḥusayn.' He used to say to Fātimah, 'Call my sons for me,' and he would breathe in their scents and embrace them to him." (Tirmidhī)

---

1. It is as stated in *al-Adab al-Mufrad* of *Imām* Bukhārī, that ʿAbdullāh ibn ʿUmar ؊ went to Makkah on *Ḥajj* in the year after al-Husain was martyred in Iraq. Someone from the people of Iraq who had also come to Makkah for *Ḥajj* visited Ibn ʿUmar and asked him what should be done if someone in the state of *iḥrām* kills a fly. Ibn ʿUmar rebuked the people of Iraq in sadness and said this.

48. Abū Sa'īd al-Khudrī ☙ related that the Messenger of Allah 🌸 said, "Al-Ḥasan and al-Ḥusayn are the lords of the young people of the Garden." (Tirmidhī)

49. 'Imrān ibn al-Ḥusayn ☙ related that the Prophet 🌸 said, " 'Alī is from me and I am from him, and he is the friend of every believer." (Tirmidhī)

50. Zayd ibn Arqam ☙ related that the Messenger of Allah 🌸 said, "If I am a person's guardian, 'Alī is also his guardian." (Tirmidhī)

51. Ibn 'Umar ☙ related that the Messenger of Allah 🌸 said to 'Alī, "You are my brother in this world and the Next." (Tirmidhī)

52. It is related that 'Ā'ishah ☙ said, "I have never been jealous about any wife of the Prophet 🌸 as I was jealous of Khadījah. She died before he married me. I used to hear him mention her and Allah commanded him to give her the good news of a house made of pearl. If he slaughtered a sheep, he would send her friends enough to suffice them." (Bukhārī)

53. 'Urwah ibn az-Zubayr related that the Prophet 🌸 said, "O Umm Salamah! Do not trouble me about 'Ā'ishah. Allah has not sent down revelation to me while I was under the blanket of any woman from among you except her." (Bukhārī)

6

LOVE FOR THE COMPANIONS OF THE PROPHET ﷺ

Allah, Exalted is He, says, *"Muhammad is the Messenger of Allah, and those who are with him are strong against unbelievers, (but) compassionate amongst each other. Thou wilt see them bow and prostrate themselves (in prayer), seeking grace from Allah and (His) Good Pleasure. On their faces are their marks, (being) the traces of their prostration. This is their similitude in the Torah, and their similitude in the Gospel is like a seed which sends forth its blade, then makes it strong; it then becomes thick, and it stands on its own stem, (filling) the sowers with wonder and delight. As a result, it fills the unbelievers with rage at them. Allah has promised those among them who believe and do righteous deeds forgiveness and a great reward."* (48: 29)

Allah ﷻ says, *"The vanguard (of Islam), the first of those who forsook (their homes) and of those who gave them aid, and (also) those who follow them in (all) good deeds – well-pleased is Allah with them, as are they with Him: for them hath He prepared gardens under which rivers flow, to dwell therein forever. That is the supreme Felicity."* (9: 100)

Allah ﷻ says, *"Not equal among you are those who spent (freely) and fought, before the Victory, (with those who did so later). Those are higher in rank than those who spent (freely) and fought afterwards. But to all Allah has promised a goodly (reward). And Allah is well-acquainted with all that ye do."* (57: 10)

54. 'Abdullāh ibn Mughaffal رضي الله عنه related that the Messenger of Allah ﷺ said, "[Fear] Allah! Allah! Concerning my Companions! Do not take them as a target after me. Whoever loves them, it is

from love of me that he loves them. Whoever hates them, it is from hatred of me that he hates them. Whoever harms them has harmed me, and whoever harms me, has harmed Allah, and whoever harms Allah is about to be seized." (Tirmidhī)

55. 'Imrān ibn al-Ḥuṣayn ﷺ related that the Messenger of Allah ﷺ said, "The best of my community are my generation and then those who follow them and then those who follow them." 'Imrān said, "I do not know whether he said it twice or three times." "Then after them will come a people who testify when they are not asked to testify, and who betray and are not trustworthy, who make a vow and do not fulfil it. Fleshiness will appear among them." (Bukhārī)

56. 'Abdullāh ibn Mas'ūd ﷺ related that the Prophet ﷺ said, "The best people are those of my generation, and then those after them, and then those after them. Then will come people whose testimony precedes their oath and whose oath precedes their testimony." (Bukhārī)

57. Abū Sa'īd al-Khudrī ﷺ related that the Messenger of Allah ﷺ said, "Do not curse my Companions. If one of you were to spend the like of Uḥud in gold, it would not reach (in reward) to a *mudd* or half a *mudd* of one of them."[1] (Bukhārī)

58. Rifā'ah ibn Rāfi' ﷺ said, "Jibrīl, peace be upon him, came to the Prophet ﷺ and said, 'How do you estimate the people of Badr among you?' He said, 'They are among the best of the Muslims,' or words to that effect. He said, 'The same applies to those angels who were present at Badr.' " (Bukhārī)

59. Ḥafṣah ﷺ reported that the Messenger of Allah ﷺ said, "I hope, Allah willing, that no one who was present at Badr and al-Ḥudaybiyyah will enter the Fire." She said, "Messenger of Allah,

1. A *mudd* is a small measurement which was used to measure grain. Its weight, compared to the metric system, is about 0.79 kg.

did not Allah Almighty say, *'Not one of you but will pass over it.'* (19: 71)?" He said, "Did you not hear Him say, 'Then We shall save those who guarded against evil'?" (Ibn Mājah) In the variant of Muslim from Umm Bishr, "Allah willing, none of the people of the Tree[2] who gave allegiance under it, will enter the Fire."

60. Jābir said, "There were 1,400 of us present on the Day of al-Ḥudaybiyyah. The Prophet said to us, 'Today you are the best people on earth.' " (Bukhārī, Muslim)

61. Al-Barā' ibn 'Āzib reported: I heard the Prophet say (about the *Anṣār*), "Only a believer loves them and only a hypocrite hates them. Allah loves anyone who loves them and Allah hates anyone who hates them." (Bukhārī)

62. Ibn 'Abbās reported that the Prophet said, "If I were to take anyone as an intimate friend, I would have taken Abū Bakr as my friend, but he is my brother and my Companion." (Bukhārī, Muslim)

63. It is reported that Abū Hurayrah said that the Prophet said, "In the nations before you there were people who were spoken to (by Allah). If there was to be such a man among my community, it would be 'Umar." (Bukhārī)

64. 'Ā'ishah reported that the Messenger of Allah said about 'Uthmān, "Shall I not be shy before a man before whom the angels are shy?" (Muslim)

65. Sa'd ibn Abī Waqqāṣ reported that the Prophet said to 'Alī "Are you not content to be in the same position in relation to me as Harun, peace be upon him, was to Mūsā, peace be upon him?" (Bukhārī)

---

2. Refers to the Tree at Ḥudaybiyyah under which the *bay'at ar-Riḍwān* took place.

66. It is reported from Anas ibn Mālik ؓ that when they were suffering from a drought, 'Umar ibn al-Khaṭṭāb ؓ prayed for rain through the intercession of 'Abbās ibn 'Abd al-Muṭṭalib ؓ. He said, " 'O Allah, we used to intercede with You through our Prophet, and You gave us rain. We intercede with You now through the uncle of Your Prophet, so give us rain!' and they had rain." (Bukhārī)

67. Jābir ؓ reported that the Messenger of Allah ﷺ said, "Every Prophet has a close disciple. My close disciple is Az-Zubayr." (Bukhārī)

68. Qays ibn Abī Ḥāzim ؓ said, "I saw the hand of Ṭalḥah paralysed. He protected the Prophet ﷺ with it on the Day of Uḥud." (Bukhārī)

69. 'Alī ibn Abī Ṭālib ؓ said, "I did not hear the Messenger of Allah ﷺ mention both his parents [showing respect] for anyone except Sa'd ibn Mālik (i.e. Sa'd ibn Abī Waqqāṣ) ؓ. He said on the Day of Uḥud, 'O Sa'd! Shoot! May my father and my mother be your ransom!' " (Bukhārī, Muslim)

70. Anas ibn Mālik ؓ reported that the Prophet ﷺ said, "Every community has a trustworthy representative, and the trustworthy representative of this community is Abū 'Ubaydah ibn al-Jarrāḥ." (Bukhārī, Muslim)

71. Ibn 'Abbās ؓ said, "The Prophet ﷺ hugged me to his chest and said, 'O Allah! Teach him wisdom!' " (Bukhārī)

72. It is reported that Ḥafṣah ؓ said that the Prophet ﷺ said to her, " 'Abdullāh (i.e. Ibn 'Umar ibn al-Khaṭṭab) is a right acting man." (Bukhārī)

73. 'Abdurraḥmān ibn Yazīd ؓ said, "We asked Ḥudhayfah ؓ to tell us who resembled the Prophet ﷺ in appearance and guidance so that we could learn from him. He said, 'I do not know of anyone closer in appearance, guidance and conduct to the Prophet ﷺ than Ibn Umm 'Abd (i.e. 'Abdullāh ibn Mas'ūd).' " (Bukhārī)

74. Jābir said: "I heard the Prophet ﷺ say, 'The Throne shook at the death of Sa'd ibn Mu'ādh.' " (Bukhārī)

75. 'Abdullāh ibn 'Umar said: "I heard the Prophet ﷺ say, 'Learn to recite the Qur'ān from four people: Ibn Mas'ūd, Sālim the *mawlā* of Abū Ḥudhayfah, Ubayy ibn Ka'b and Mu'ādh ibn Jabal.' " (Bukhārī)

76. Sa'd ibn Abī Waqqāṣ said, "I did not hear the Prophet ﷺ say about anyone walking on the earth that he was one of the people of the Garden except 'Abdullāh ibn Salām." (Bukhārī)

77. It is reported from 'Ā'ishah that the Quraysh were concerned about the case of the Makhzūmī woman. They said, "Who will dare to speak to him except Usāmah ibn Zayd, the beloved of the Messenger of Allah ﷺ?" (Bukhārī)

78. Al-Barā' ibn 'Āzib reported that the Prophet ﷺ said to Ja'far ibn Abī Ṭālib, "You resemble me physically and in terms of character." (Tirmidhī)

7

LOVE FOR THE SAKE OF ALLAH سبحانه وتعالى AND HATRED FOR THE SAKE OF ALLAH سبحانه وتعالى

Allah, Exalted is He, says, *"Thou wilt not find any people who believe in Allah and the Last Day, loving those who resist Allah and His Messenger, even though they were their fathers or their sons, or their brothers, or their kindred. For such He has written faith in their hearts, and strengthened them with a spirit from Himself. And He will admit them to gardens beneath which rivers flow, to dwell therein (forever). Allah will be well pleased with them, and they with Him."* (58: 22)

He سبحانه وتعالى said, *"Your (real) friends are (no less than) Allah, His Messenger, and the (fellowship of) believers – those who establish regular prayers and regular charity. And they bow down humbly (in worship)."* (5: 55)

He سبحانه وتعالى says: *"Let not the believers take for friends or helpers unbelievers rather than believers: if any do that, in nothing will there be help from Allah: except by way of precaution, that ye may guard yourselves from them."* (3: 28)

79. It is reported from Abū Hurayrah رضي الله عنه that the Messenger of Allah ﷺ said, "Allah Almighty will say on the Day of Rising, 'Where are those who loved one another for the sake of My majesty? Today I will shade them in My shade on a day when there is no shade but My shade." (Muslim)

80. Mu'ādh ibn Jabal رضي الله عنه reported: "I heard the Messenger of Allah ﷺ say, 'Allah Almighty said, "My love is mandatory for those

who love each other for My sake and those who sit with each other for My sake, and those who visit each other for My sake and those who give to each other generously for My sake." ' " (Mālik; in *al-Muwaṭṭā'*)

81. Abū Hurayrah ؓ reported that the Messenger of Allah ﷺ said, "A man visited a brother of his in another town and Allah appointed an angel to wait for him on his way. When he came to him, the angel said, 'Where are you going?' He said, 'I am going to a brother of mine in this town.' He said, 'Do you have some property with him that you want to check on?' He said, 'No, it is only that I love him for the sake of Allah Almighty.' He said, 'I am a messenger of Allah to you to tell you that Allah loves you as you love this man for His sake.' " (Muslim)

82. Anas ؓ reported that the Prophet ﷺ said, "Anyone who possesses three attributes will experience the sweetness of belief: that he loves Allah and His Messenger more than anything else; that he loves someone for the sake of Allah alone; and that he hates the idea of reverting to disbelief as much as he would hate being thrown into a fire." (Bukhārī, Muslim)

83. Abū Hurayrah ؓ reported that the Messenger of Allah ﷺ said, "There are seven whom Allah will shade with His shade on the day when there is no shade but His shade: a just Imām (ruler), a youth who grows up worshipping Allah, the Mighty and Exalted, a man whose heart is attached to the mosque, two men who love each other for the sake of Allah, meeting and parting for that reason alone, a man who refuses the advances of a noble and beautiful woman, saying, 'I fear Allah', a man who gives *ṣadaqah* and conceals it so that his left hand does not know what his right hand gives, and a man who remembers Allah when he is alone and his eyes overflow with tears." (Bukhārī, Muslim)

84. It is reported from Abū Dharr ؓ that the Messenger of Allah ﷺ said, "Anyone who loves for the sake of Allah and hates for the sake of Allah and gives for the sake of Allah and withholds for the sake of Allah, has perfect belief." (Abū Dāwūd)

85. Abū Umāmah 🌸 reported that the Messenger of Allah 🌸 said, "The best of actions is love for the sake of Allah and hate for the sake of Allah." (Abū Dāwūd)

86. Abū Hurayrah 🌸 reported that the Messenger of Allah 🌸 said, "If anyone visits someone who is ill or visits a brother of his in Islam, a caller calls to him, 'You are good and your walking was good and you made your place in the Garden.' " (Tirmidhī)

87. Al-Miqdām ibn Ma'dīkarib 🌸 said, "If a man loves his brother, he should tell him that he loves him." (Tirmidhī)

8

RESPECT FOR THE SANCTITY OF MUSLIMS

Allah, Exalted is He, says: *"O ye who believe! Let not some men among you mock others. It may be that the (latter) are better than the (former): nor let some women mock others: it may be that the (latter) are better than the (former). Nor defame nor be sarcastic to each other, nor call each other by (offensive) nicknames. Ill-seeming is a name connoting wickedness, (to be used by one) after he has believed."* (49: 11)

He says: *"Avoid suspicion as much (as possible), for suspicion in some cases is a sin, and spy not on each other, nor speak ill of each other behind their backs. Would any of you like to eat the flesh of his dead brother? Nay, ye would abhor it."* (49: 12)

He says: *"And those who annoy believing men and women undeservedly, bear (on themselves) a calumny and a glaring sin."* (33: 58)

He says: *"If anyone slew a person – unless it be for murder or for spreading mischief in the land – it would be as if he slew the whole people and if anyone saved a life, it would be as if he saved the life of the whole people."* (5: 32)

88. Ibn 'Abbās reported that the Messenger of Allah ﷺ addressed the people on the Day of Sacrifice (at Minā on the tenth of Dhu'l Ḥijjah during his farewell pilgrimage) and said, "O people! What day is this?" They said, "A sacred day." He said, "And what place is this?" They said, "A sacred place." He said, "And what month is this?" They said, "A sacred month." He said, "Your blood, your property and your honour are sacred to you like the sacredness of this day in

this place in this month." He repeated this several times and then he lifted his head and said, "O Allah, have I conveyed it? O Allah, have I conveyed it?" Ibn 'Abbās said, "By the One who has my soul in His hand, it was his legacy to his community: 'Let those who are present convey it to those who are absent. Do not revert to being as unbelievers after I have gone, cutting each other's throats.' " (Bukhārī)

89. Yazīd ibn Sharīk, may Allah have mercy on him, said, "I saw 'Alī ♦ speaking on the *minbar* and I heard him say, 'No, by Allah, we have no other book which we read except the Book of Allah and what is in these pages.' He made them public and they dealt with the ages of camels concerning the blood money and some legal instructions on retaliation or compensation for criminal injuries; and in it that the Messenger of Allah ♦ said, 'The power of the Muslims to grant protection applies to all. It can be granted by the least of them. If anyone betrays a Muslim, on him rests the curse of Allah, and that of the angels, and all people. Allah will not accept any recompense or ransom from him on the Day of Rising.' " (Muslim)

90. Abū Mūsā al-Ash'arī ♦ said that the Messenger of Allah ♦ said, "A believer in respect of another believer is like a building whose parts support one another." (Bukhārī, Muslim)

91. An-Nu'mān ibn Bashīr ♦ reported that the Messenger of Allah ♦ said, "The likeness of the believers in their mutual love, mercy and affection is that of the body. When one limb of it complains, the rest of the body reacts with sleeplessness and fever." (Bukhārī, Muslim)

92. Ibn 'Umar ♦ reported that the Messenger of Allah ♦ said, "The Muslim is the brother of the Muslim. He should not wrong him or surrender him to his enemy or leave him to perish unsupported. Allah will take care of the needs of anyone who takes care of the needs of his brother. On the Day of Rising, Allah will dispel the anxiety of anyone who dispels the anxiety of another Muslim. On the Day of Rising, Allah will veil anyone who veils another Muslim." (Bukhārī, Muslim)

93. Abū Hurayrah ﷺ reported that the Messenger of Allah ﷺ said, "Do not envy one another, do not bid against one another, (bidding just to raise the price when one has no intention of buying in order to deceive the customer), do not hate one another, do not turn your backs on one another, and none of you should sell against the sale of anyone else. Be slaves of Allah, as brothers. The Muslim is the brother of the Muslim: he should not wrong him, leave him unsupported nor scorn him nor disappoint him. Fear of Allah is here," and he pointed to his breast three times. "It is enough evil for a man to scorn his Muslim brother. Everything of a Muslim is sacred to another Muslim, his blood, property and honour." (Muslim)

94. Abū Hurayrah ﷺ reported that the Messenger of Allah ﷺ said, "Beware of opinion. Opinion is the falsest kind of speech. Do not spy or pry. Do not be rivals or envy one another. Do not hate one another or show enmity to one another. Do not turn your backs on one another. Slaves of Allah, be as brothers." (Muslim)

95. Abū Ayyūb al-Anṣārī ﷺ said that the Messenger of Allah ﷺ said, "It is not lawful for a Muslim to cut himself off from his brother for more than three nights so that when they meet, this one turns aside and that one turns aside. The best of the two[1] is the one who greets the other first." (Bukhārī).

96. Jābir ﷺ said: "I heard the Messenger of Allah ﷺ say, 'The Muslim is the one from whose tongue and hand other Muslims are safe.' " (Muslim)

97. Ibn 'Umar ﷺ reported that the Prophet ﷺ said in the Farewell Ḥajj, "Woe to you! (or Bother you!) Do not revert to being as unbelievers after I have gone, cutting each other's throats." (Muslim)

---

1. *Imām* Nawawī said that to cut oneself off from a Muslim for more than three days is prohibited by the clear order of the *Sharī'ah*. For less than three is forgiven, since human beings are created with the attribute of anger, which may take time to overcome.

98. Ibn Mas'ūd ﷺ reported that the Messenger of Allah ﷺ said, "Cursing a Muslim is iniquity and killing him is disbelief." (Muslim)

99. Abū Umāmah ﷺ reported that the Messenger of Allah ﷺ said, "Allah has made the Fire mandatory and forbidden the Garden to anyone who takes the right of a Muslim man through an oath." A man said to him, "Even if it is something insignificant?" He said, "Even if it is a twig of *arak* (a bush)." (Muslim)

100. Abū Hurayrah ﷺ reported that the Messenger of Allah ﷺ said, "The angels curse anyone who points a sharp iron implement at his brother (Muslim) until he stops doing that, even if it is his full brother."[2] (Muslim)

101. Sa'īd ibn Zayd ﷺ reported that the Prophet ﷺ said, "One of the worst forms of usury is detracting from a Muslim's honour without legal right." (Abū Dāwūd)

102. Anas ibn Mālik ﷺ reported that the Messenger of Allah ﷺ said, "When I ascended through the heavens, I passed by some people holding copper nails with which they were gouging their faces and chests. I said, 'Who are these, Jibril?' He said, 'Those are the people who consumed people's flesh (by back-biting and tale bearing) and attacked their honour.' " (Abū Dāwūd)

103. Abū Barzah al-Aslamī ﷺ reported that the Messenger of Allah ﷺ said, "O company of those who express belief with their tongues when belief has not entered their hearts! Do not slander the Muslims! Do not seek out their faults! If anyone seeks out their faults, Allah, the Mighty and Majestic, will seek out his faults and anyone whose faults Allah seeks out will be disgraced and humiliated in his own house." (Abū Dāwūd)

104. Mu'ādh ibn Anas al-Juhanī reported that his father said that the Messenger of Allah ﷺ said, "If anyone protects a believer from

2. Meaning that even as a joke it is unlawful (prohibited).

a hypocrite," I think he said, "Allah will send an angel to protect his flesh from the fire of *Jahannam* on the Day of Rising. If anyone imputes something to a Muslim desiring to disgrace him, Allah will detain him on the bridge of *Jahannam* until he retracts what he said." (Abū Dāwūd)

105. Jābir ibn 'Abdullāh and Abū Ṭalḥah Zayd ibn Sahl al-Anṣārī, may Allah be pleased with them, reported that the Messenger of Allah ﷺ said, "No man forsakes a Muslim in a place in which his respect is defamed and his honour disparaged without Allah, the Mighty and Majestic, forsaking him in a place where he desires His help. No man helps a Muslim in a place in which his honour is disparaged and his respect defamed without Allah, the Mighty and Majestic, helping him in a place where he desires His help." (Abū Dāwūd)

106. Nāfi', may Allah have mercy on him, said that one day 'Abdullāh ibn 'Umar ﵁ looked at the House, and said, "How immense you are and how immense your sanctity is, but the sanctity of the believer is greater in the sight of Allah than yours." (Tirmidhī)

9

EARNING A LIVELIHOOD
AND MANUAL LABOUR

Allah, Exalted is He, says, *"And when the prayer is finished, then may ye disperse through the land, and seek of the bounty of Allah."* (62: 10)

He ﷻ says: *"It is no crime in you if ye seek of the bounty of your Lord (during pilgrimage)."* (2: 198)

He ﷻ says, *"Allah hath permitted trade and forbidden usury."* (2: 275)

He ﷻ says: *"Eat up not your property among yourselves in vanities; but let there be amongst you traffic and trade by mutual good-will."* (4: 29)

He ﷻ says: *"And thou seest the ships therein that plough the waves, that ye may seek (thus) of the bounty of Allah."* (35: 12)

He ﷻ says: *"By men whom neither traffic nor merchandise can divert from the Remembrance of Allah."* (24: 37)

He ﷻ says: *"O ye who believe! Give of the good things which ye have (honourably) earned, and of the fruits of the earth which We have produced for you."* (2: 267)

107. Az-Zubayr ibn al-'Awwām ؓ reported that the Messenger of Allah ﷺ said, "It is better for one of you to take some rope, and go to a mountain and bring a bundle of firewood on his back and sell it by which Allah saves his honour and dignity, than for him to ask people who then give to him or refuse." (Bukhārī)

108. Abū Hurayrah ﷺ reported that the Messenger of Allah ﷺ said, "It is better for you to carry a bundle of firewood on your back than to go and beg from someone who might then give to you or refuse to give you anything." (Bukhārī, Muslim)

109. Al-Miqdām ibn Ma'dīkarib ﷺ reported that the Prophet ﷺ said, "No one eats any better food than a man who eats from the work of his own hands. The Prophet Dāwūd, peace be upon him, used to eat from the work of his own hands." (Bukhārī)

110. Abū Hurayrah ﷺ reported that the Messenger of Allah ﷺ said, "Zakariyyā, peace be upon him, was a carpenter." (Muslim)

111. 'Ubaydullāh ibn 'Adī ﷺ reported that two men told him that they went to the Messenger of Allah ﷺ and asked him for *ṣadaqah*. He looked at them and saw that they were sturdy and said, "If you wish I will give to you but there is no good in it for the wealthy or those who are strong enough to earn." (Abū Dāwūd, an-Nasā'ī)

112. 'Abdullāh ibn 'Amr ibn al-'Āṣ ﷺ reported that the Messenger of Allah ﷺ said, "Anyone who takes charge of an orphan's wealth should trade and not leave it so that *ṣadaqah* consumes it." (Tirmidhī)

113. 'Abdullāh ibn 'Abbās ﷺ said, " 'Ukāẓ, Mejannah and Dhu'l-Majāz were markets of the people in the time of *Jāhiliyyah*. When Islam came, it seemed that people regarded trading in the seasons (of pilgrimage) as wrong action until it was revealed, 'It is no crime in you if you seek of the bounty of your Lord.' " (2: 198) Ibn 'Abbās recited it (commenting) that it is during *Ḥajj* seasons. (Bukhārī)

114. 'Abdurraḥmān ibn 'Awf ﷺ said, "The Messenger of Allah ﷺ established brotherhood between me and Sa'd ibn ar-Rabī'. Sa'd ibn ar-Rabī' said, 'I am the wealthiest man of the *Anṣār* so I will allot you half of my property. See which of my two wives you like best and I will divorce her for you. When she has become lawful (completed her '*iddah*), then you can marry her.' 'Abdurraḥmān said, 'That is not what I need. Is there any market

where trading goes on?' He said, 'The Qaynuqa' market.' " 'Abdurraḥmān went there and bought some dried yoghurt and ghee. Then he continued to go (and trade). It was not long before 'Abdurraḥmān arrived with traces of yellow scent on him. The Messenger of Allah ﷺ asked, "Have you got married?" He said, "Yes." He said, "To whom?" He said, "A woman of the *Anṣār*." He said, "How much did you give her?" He said, "Gold the weight of a date-stone (or a date-stone of gold)." The Prophet ﷺ said to him, "Hold a wedding-feast, even if only with a sheep." (Bukhārī)

115. Abū Hurayrah ؓ said, "You say that Abū Hurayrah relates many *aḥādīth* from the Messenger of Allah ﷺ and you say, 'Why do the *Muhājirūn* and *Anṣār* not relate from the Messenger of Allah ﷺ as Abū Hurayrah does?' My brothers among the *Muhājirūn* used to be busy with business in the markets while I used to stick close to the Messenger of Allah ﷺ (content) with just enough to fill my stomach. I was present when they were absent and I remembered when they forgot. My brothers among the *Anṣār* were busy with their property while I was one of the poor people of the *Ṣuffah*.[1] I would remember when they forgot." (Bukhārī)

116. 'Ā'ishah ؓ said, "When Abū Bakr as-Ṣiddīq ؓ was appointed Caliph, he said, 'My people know that my profession was quite sufficient to provide for my family. But now I am busy with the affairs of the Muslims, so let the family of Abū Bakr eat from this (public) property, while he employs and devotes his professional expertise for Muslims.' " (Bukhārī)

117. Al-Barā' ibn 'Āzib and Zayd ibn Arqam ؓ said, "We used to be merchants during the time of the Messenger of Allah ﷺ and we asked the Messenger of Allah ﷺ about money exchange, and he said, 'There is no harm if it is hand to hand business. If there is a delay (from any side), then it is not permissible.' " (Bukhārī)

---

1. *Ṣuffah* was a place in the Mosque of the Prophet ﷺ where the new Muslims, and seekers of knowledge who were without families, were staying. They sought only to learn and worship as they saw the Prophet ﷺ do or teach.

118. Ḥudhayfah ﷺ said, "One of the slaves of Allah Almighty to whom Allah gave money will be brought before Him and He will say to him, 'What did you do in the world?' He will say – and they cannot conceal anything from Allah – 'O my Lord, You gave me wealth and I used to do business with people. Part of my character was excusing others. I used to be easy with those who were wealthy and give time to pay to those in difficulties.' Allah Almighty will say, 'I have more right to do that than you. Pardon My slave.' " 'Uqbah ibn 'Āmr and Abū Mas'ūd al-Anṣārī ﷺ said: "This is how we heard it from the mouth of the Messenger of Allah ﷺ." (Muslim)

119. Abū Hurayrah ﷺ reported that the Messenger of Allah ﷺ passed by a heap of grain and put his hand in it and his fingers felt moistness. He said, "You with the grain, what is this?" He said, "The rain caught it, Messenger of Allah." He said, "So why didn't you put it at the top so that people could see it? Anyone who cheats is not one of us." (Muslim)

120. Ḥakīm ibn Ḥizām ﷺ reported that the Messenger of Allah ﷺ said, "The seller and the buyer have the option (to revoke) as long as they have not separated (or he said, 'until they separate'). If they speak the truth and make things clear, they will be blessed in their sale. If they conceal and lie, they may earn some profit but the blessing of their transaction will be wiped out." (Bukhārī, Muslim)

121. Rifā'ah ibn Rāfi' ﷺ reported that the Messenger of Allah ﷺ said, "Merchants will be raised up on the Day of Rising as profligates except those who are fearful of Allah, do good, and tell the truth." (Tirmidhī)

122. Anas ibn Mālik ﷺ said, "There is no Muslim who plants a tree or sows a crop from which birds, man or beasts eat but that it is *ṣadaqah* for him." (Bukhārī, Muslim)

123. Ibn 'Umar ﷺ said that the Prophet ﷺ employed the Jews of Khaybar to work the land in return for half of its produce of fruit

or other crops. He used to give his wives a hundred *wasq*[2] each, eighty *wasq* of dates and twenty *wasq* of barley. When 'Umar divided up Khaybar, he gave the wives of the Prophet ﷺ a choice between ownership of land and water, or continuing as before. Some chose the land and some chose the *wasq*. 'Ā'ishah chose the land. (Bukhārī)

124. 'Amr ibn Dīnār al-Makkī said, "I said to Ṭāwūs, 'I wish you would give up cropsharing since they claim that the Prophet ﷺ forbade it.' He said, "Amr! I give them land and help them. The most knowledgeable of them, i.e. Ibn 'Abbās ؓ told me that the Prophet ﷺ did not forbid it, but said, "It is better for one of you to give land to his brother than to take a fixed rent for it." ' " (Bukhārī)

2. A *wasq* is sixty *sa'*. A *sa'* is a measurement approximately equal in metric weight to 3 1/6 kg.

10

REFRAINING FROM ASKING (OTHERS) AND MODERATION IN SEEKING A LIVELIHOOD

Allah, Exalted is He, says: *"There is no moving creature on earth but its sustenance dependeth on Allah."* (11: 6)

He 🕮 says: *"(Charity is) for those in need, who, in Allah's cause are restricted (from travel), and cannot move about in the land, seeking (for trade or work): the ignorant man thinks, because of their modesty, that they are free from want. Thou shalt know them by their (unfailing) mark: they beg not importunately from all and sundry."* (2: 273)

He 🕮 says: *"Those who, when they spend, are not extravagant and not niggardly, but hold a just (balance) between those (extremes)."* (25: 67)

He 🕮 says, *"I have only created jinns and men, that they may serve Me. No Sustenance do I require of them, nor do I require that they should feed Me. Lo! Allah, is He that giveth livelihood the Lord of unbreakable might."* (51: 56–58)

125. Ḥakīm ibn Ḥizām 🕮 reported that the Messenger of Allah (🕮) said, "This wealth is verdant and sweet. Anyone who takes it in a generous spirit will be blessed in it but anyone who takes it in an avaricious way will not be blessed in it, like someone who eats and is not satisfied. The upper hand (he who gives) is better than the lower hand (he who takes)." (Bukhārī, Muslim)

126. Abū Saʿīd al-Khudrī 🕮 reported that the Messenger of Allah (🕮) said, "This wealth is verdant and sweet. Everything that grows

in the spring kills by distending the stomach, or nearly so, apart from the animal that eats *khaḍirah*[1] – it eats until its sides fill out, then faces towards the sun, chews the cud, defecates loosely and urinates, and then starts eating again. This wealth is sweet: for anyone who acquires it rightfully and disposes of it rightfully, it is an excellent support; whoever acquires it wrongfully is [like] someone who eats but is never satisfied." (Bukhārī)

127. Al-Miswar ibn Makhramah ⬥ reported that the Messenger of Allah ⬥ said, "By Allah, it is not poverty I fear for you. What I fear for you is that this world will be expanded for you as it was expanded for those before you and then you will contend over it as they contended for it and it will distract you as it distracted them." (Bukhārī)

128. Abū Hurayrah ⬥ reported that the Messenger of Allah ⬥ said, "May the slave of the *dīnār* and the *dirham*, the *qaṭīfah*[2] (velvet garment) and *khamīṣah*[3] (expensive black cloak) perish! If he is given them he is pleased, and if he is not given them he is not pleased." (Bukhārī)

129. Anas ibn Mālik and 'Abdullāh ibn 'Abbās, may Allah be pleased with them, reported that the Messenger of Allah ⬥ said, "If the son of Ādam were to have a valley full of gold, he would want to have two valleys; and his mouth will only be filled by dust. Allah turns to whoever turns in repentance." (Bukhārī, Muslim)

130. 'Abdullāh ibn 'Amr ibn al-'Āṣ ⬥ reported that the Messenger of Allah ⬥ used to give 'Umar a gift and he would say, "Give it to someone poorer than me!" He would say, "Take it and make use of it or give it as *ṣadaqah*. Take what comes to you of this wealth when you are not greedy (longing to have it) or begging, but do not let yourself pursue wealth." (Muslim)

---

1. A tall, rough, green plant with leaves like those of pearl millet.
2-3. Symbols of expensive clothes and dress which people boast about.

131. Ibn 'Amr reported that the Messenger of Allah said, "The successful man is he who becomes a Muslim, has adequate provision and whom Allah makes satisfied with what He gives him." (Muslim)

132. Jābir reported that the Messenger of Allah said, "O people! Fear Allah and be moderate in seeking a livelihood. No self will die until it has received its full provision, even if it is slow in coming. Fear Allah and be moderate in seeking. Take what is lawful and leave what is unlawful." (Ibn Mājah)

133. Abū Hurayrah reported that the Prophet said, "Wealth does not consist in having a lot of goods. Wealth consists in the richness of the self." (Bukhārī, Muslim)

134. Ibn 'Umar said, "The Messenger of Allah took hold of my shoulders and said, 'Be in this world as if you were a stranger or a wayfarer.' " (Bukhārī)

135. Sahl ibn Sa'd reported that the Messenger of Allah said, "Make do with little of this world and Allah will love you and make do with little of what belongs to other people and people will love you." (Ibn Mājah)

136. Abū Hurayrah reported that the Messenger of Allah said, "The slave says, 'My property! My property! But he has only three things from his property: what he eats and is used up, what he wears and is worn out, and what he gives away and thus gains. Everything other than that is left behind and he bequeathes it to people." (Muslim)

137. Abū Barzah al-Aslamī reported that the Prophet said, "A slave will be kept standing on the day of Judgement until he is asked about his life and how he spent it, his knowledge and how he acted upon it, his property and how he acquired it and spent it, and his body and how he wore it out." (Tirmidhī)

I I

ON SPENDING IN GOOD WAYS

Allah, Exalted is He, says: *"Do ye spend in the least (in His Cause), but He replaces it."* (34: 39)

He 🕮 says, *"Whatever of good ye give benefits your own souls, and ye shall only do so seeking the 'Face' of Allah. Whatever good ye give, shall be rendered back to you, and ye shall not be dealt with unjustly."* (2: 272)

He 🕮 says, *"And whatever of good ye give, be assured Allah knoweth it well."* (2: 273)

138. Jarīr ibn 'Abdullāh 🕮 said, "Once we were with the Messenger of Allah 🕮 at the beginning of the day when some people came, barefoot, wearing striped garments or cloaks, girded with swords. Most of them were from Mudar. The face of the Messenger of Allah 🕮 changed because of his concern at what he saw of their extreme need. He went inside and then came out and commanded Bilāl to give the *adhān* and the *iqāmah*. He prayed and then recited, *'O mankind! fear your Guardian Lord, who created you from a single person, created, out of it, his mate, and from them twain scattered (like seeds) countless men and women; — fear Allah, through Whom ye demand your mutual (rights), and be heedful of the wombs (that bore you): for Allah ever watches over you.'* (4: 1) and another verse which is at the end of Sūrah al-Ḥashr, *'O you who believe! Fear Allah, and let every soul look to what (provision) it has sent forth for the morrow.'* (59: 18) (And said) 'Let a man give from his *dīnār* and his *dirham*, from his clothes, from the *ṣāʿ* of his wheat, from the *ṣāʿ* of his dates,' until he said, 'even if it is a half of a date.' A man of the *Anṣār* brought a bag which he could barely get his arms round, indeed, he could not carry it.

Then the people came one after another until I saw two heaps of food and clothes and I saw the face of the Messenger of Allah ﷺ shining as if it was illuminated. The Messenger of Allah ﷺ said, 'Anyone who initiates a good *sunnah* in Islam has its reward and the reward of whoever does it after him without that decreasing their reward in any way. Anyone who creates a bad *sunnah* in Islam bears its burden and the burden of whoever acts by it after him without that decreasing their burden in any way.' " (Muslim)

139. Abū Dharr ﷺ said, "I came to the Prophet ﷺ while he was sitting in the shade of the Ka'bah. When he saw me, he said, 'They are truly the losers, by the Lord of the Ka'bah!' " He said, "I went and sat down. I could not stay for long so I got up and said, 'Messenger of Allah, my mother and father be your ransom! Who are they?' He said, 'They are those who have a lot of wealth except for the one who spends like this and like that, before him and behind him, to his right and to his left. Very few are they!' " (Muslim)

140. Ibn Mas'ūd ﷺ reported that the Prophet ﷺ said, "There is no envy except with regard to two things: a man to whom Allah has given wealth and empowered him to spend for the truth, and a man to whom Allah has given wisdom and he acts by it and teaches it." (Bukhārī, Muslim)

141. Ibn Mas'ūd ﷺ reported that the Messenger of Allah ﷺ said, "Which of you loves the property of his heir more than he loves his own property?" They said, "O Messenger of Allah, there is none of us who does not love his own property more." He said, "His property is what he sends ahead, and the property of his heir is what he leaves behind." (Bukhārī)

142. Abū Hurayrah ﷺ reported that the Messenger of Allah ﷺ said, "Whoever gives in *ṣadaqah* as much as a date from honest earnings – and Allah only accepts what is good – Allah will accept it in His right hand and will then increase it in size for the giver, just like one of you might rear a foal, until it becomes the size of a mountain." (Bukhārī, Muslim)

143. Abū Umāmah ⏾ reported that the Messenger of Allah ⏾ said, "O son of Ādam, it is better for you to spend what is in excess of your needs and worse for you to keep it. You will not be blamed for (keeping) enough to cover your needs. Begin with your immediate dependants. The upper hand is better than the lower hand." (Muslim)

144. 'Ā'ishah ⏾ reported that they sacrificed a sheep and the Prophet ⏾ said, "What remains of it?" She said, "Only its shoulder remains." He said, "Rather all of it except its shoulder remains."[1] (Tirmidhī)

145. Asmā' bint Abī Bakr ⏾ said, "The Messenger of Allah ⏾ told me, 'Do not withhold or it will be withheld from you.'" In one variant: "Spend, (or give out or expend) and do not hold back, or Allah will hold back from you. Do not count up what you have or Allah will count up what you owe Him. Do not refuse to spend your surplus or Allah will deny you His." (Bukhārī, Muslim)

146. Abū Hurayrah ⏾ reported that the Messenger of Allah ⏾ said, "Ṣadaqah does not decrease wealth in any way, and for pardoning someone Allah only increases a slave in might, and no one is humble for Allah's sake, without Allah, the Mighty and Majestic, elevating him." (Muslim)

147. Abū Hurayrah ⏾ also said, "A man came to the Prophet ⏾ and said, 'O Messenger of Allah, which ṣadaqah has the greatest reward?' He said, 'That you give ṣadaqah while you are healthy yet tight-fisted, in fear of poverty and desiring wealth. Do not put it off until death is near and you say, "So-and-so should have this much and so-and-so this much,"' when it already belongs to someone else." (Bukhārī, Muslim)

148. 'Uqbah ibn al-Ḥārith ⏾ said, "I prayed 'Aṣr behind the Prophet ⏾ in Madīnah. He said the salām and then got up

---

1. Everything spent and eaten in a good way is like a saving and what remains is not a saving unless given in charity or eaten by the family, which is also a reward.

hurriedly and stepped over people's shoulders making for the room of one of his wives. The people were alarmed at his speed. He came out to them and saw that they were surprised at his speed and said, 'I remembered a piece of gold that we had and I did not want it to distract me so I ordered that it be distributed.' " (Bukhārī)

149. Abū Hurayrah ﷺ reported that the Messenger of Allah ﷺ said, "A man said, 'I must give some *ṣadaqah*,' and went out with his *ṣadaqah*, putting it in the hand of a thief. The next day people said he had given *ṣadaqah* to a thief. He said, 'O Allah, praise is Yours. I will again give *ṣadaqah*.' He went out with his *ṣadaqah* and this time put it in the hand of an adulteress. The next day people said he had given *ṣadaqah* in the night to an adulteress. He said, 'O Allah, praise is Yours. I gave it to an adulteress. I will give more *ṣadaqah*.' He went out with his *ṣadaqah* and put it in the hand of a rich man. The next day people said he had given *ṣadaqah* to a rich man. He said, 'O Allah, praise is Yours. I have given *ṣadaqah* to a thief, an adulteress, and a rich man.' Then someone came and said to him,[2] 'Your *ṣadaqah* to a thief might make him abstain from stealing. What you gave to the adulteress might make her abstain from her fornication. And what you gave to the rich man might make him reflect so that he will spend from what Allah has given him.' " (Bukhārī)

2. It was in a dream, or he heard the voice of an angel announcing it, or the prophet of that time informed him.

12

PREFERRING OTHERS AND CONSOLATION

Allah, Exalted is He, says, *"But they give them preference over themselves, even though poverty was their (own lot)."* (59: 9)

He ﷻ says: *"And they feed, for the love of Allah, the indigent, the orphan, and the captive, saying, 'We feed you for the sake of Allah alone. No reward do we desire from you, nor thanks.'"* (76: 8–9)

He ﷻ says: *"But those most devoted to Allah shall be removed far from it – those who spend their wealth for increase – in self-purification and have in their minds no favour from anyone for which a reward is expected in return, but only the desire to seek the Countenance of their Lord Most High."* (92: 17–20)

He ﷻ says: *"By no means shall ye attain righteousness unless ye give (freely) of that which ye love; and whatever ye give, of a truth Allah knoweth it well."* (3: 92)

150. Abū Hurayrah ؓ said, "A man came to the Prophet ﷺ and said, 'I am famished.' He ﷺ sent for one of his wives and she said, 'By the One who sent you with the truth, I have nothing but water.' Then he sent for another and she said the same thing, until they had all said the same thing: 'By the One who sent you with the truth, I have nothing but water.' He said, 'Who will give hospitality tonight?' A man of the *Anṣār* said, 'I will, Messenger of Allah.' He took him to his place and said to his wife, 'Honour the guest of the Messenger of Allah ﷺ.' " In one variant, "He said to his wife, 'Do you have anything?' She said, 'No, only the children's food.' He said, 'Divert them with something else. When they want supper,

put them to sleep. When our guest comes in, put out the lamp and we will pretend that we are eating.' So they sat down and the guest ate and they spent the night hungry. In the morning, the man went to the Prophet ﷺ and he said, 'Allah was pleased with what you did with your guest last night.' " (Bukhārī, Muslim)

151. Sahl ibn Sa'd ؓ said, "A woman brought the Prophet ﷺ a woven cloak with a border and said, 'I wove it with my own hands so that you could wear it.' The Prophet ﷺ took it as he was in need of it. He came out to us using it as a waist-wrapper. Someone admired it and said, 'Give it to me to wear. How beautiful it is!' He said, 'Yes,' and the Prophet sat down in the assembly and then went back and folded it and sent it to him. The people said, 'You have not acted rightly. The Prophet ﷺ wore it out of need for it and then you asked him for it knowing that he never refuses a request.' He said, 'By Allah, I have not asked for it in order to wear it, but I have asked for it only so that it can be my shroud.' " Sahl said, "It was indeed his shroud." (Bukhārī)

152. Abū Sa'īd al-Khudrī ؓ said, "Once when we were on a journey with the Prophet ﷺ a man came on a camel of his and began to look to his right and left. The Messenger of Allah ﷺ said, 'Anyone who has a spare mount should prepare it for someone who does not have a mount to ride, and anyone who has extra provision should prepare it for someone who does not have any provision,' and he mentioned the different categories of property until we thought that none of us had any right to anything in excess of our needs (but must give it to someone in need of it)." (Muslim)

153. Abū Mūsā ؓ reported that the Messenger of Allah ﷺ said about the Ash'arites when they ran short of food while on a raid and when their families in Madīnah ran short of food, they gathered together what they had in one cloth and then divided it among themselves equally using the same container: "These people are from me and I am from them." (Bukhārī, Muslim)

154. Jābir ؓ reported that the Prophet ﷺ said, "The food of one person is enough for two, food for two is enough for four, and food for four is enough for eight." (Muslim)

13

ADVISING OTHERS AND DIRECTING THEM TO GOOD

Allah, Exalted is He, says reporting about Nūh, peace be upon him, *"Sincere is my advice to you."* (7: 62)

And about Hūd, peace be upon him: *"I am to you a sincere and trustworthy adviser."* (7: 68)

He ﷻ says: *"The Believers are but a single brotherhood."* (49: 10)

He ﷻ says: *"Do good that ye may prosper."* (22: 77)

155. Tamīm ibn Aws ad-Dārī ؓ reported that the Prophet ﷺ said, "The *dīn* is sincere advice." We said, "To whom?" He said, "To Allah, His Book, His Messenger, the Imāms of the Muslims and their common people." (Muslim)

156. Jarīr ibn 'Abdullāh ؓ said, "I gave allegiance to the Prophet ﷺ on the basis of performing the prayer, paying the *zakāh* and sincere advice to every Muslim." (Bukhārī, Muslim)

157. Ziyād ibn 'Alāqah said: "I heard Jarīr ibn 'Abdullāh ؓ say, 'I went to the Messenger of Allah ﷺ and I said, "I will give allegiance to you in Islam", so he imposed conditions on me, sincere advice for every Muslim. I gave allegiance to him on that basis. By the Lord of this Mosque, I am a sincere adviser to you!' " (Bukhārī)

158. Anas ibn Malīk ؓ reported that the Prophet ﷺ said, "None of you truly believes until he wants for his brother what he wants for himself." (Bukhārī, Muslim)

159. Abū Hurayrah ﷺ reported that the Prophet ﷺ said, "The rights a Muslim has over another Muslim are six: When he meets him, he should greet him. When he invites him, he should accept. When he asks his advice, he should give it to him sincerely. When he sneezes and praises Allah, he should pray for mercy for him. When he is ill, he should visit him. When he dies, he should follow his funeral procession." (Muslim)

160. Abū Hurayrah ﷺ reported that the Prophet ﷺ said, "Allah will relieve anyone, who relieves a believer of one of the afflictions of this world, from the affliction of the Day of Rising. Allah will give ease in this world and the Next to anyone who eases the hardship of another. Allah will help His slave as long as His slave is helping his brother." (Muslim)

161. Anas ibn Mālik ﷺ reported that the Messenger of Allah ﷺ said, "Help your brother, wrongdoing or wronged." A man said, "Messenger of Allah, I can help him if he is wronged but tell me how I can help him if he is wrongdoing?" He said, "You can restrain him – or prevent him – from injustice. That is helping him." (Bukhārī)

162. Abū Mūsā ﷺ reported that the Prophet ﷺ said, "Every Muslim should give *ṣadaqah*." He said, "What about someone who has nothing to give?" He said, "He should get work and earn something and give *ṣadaqah*." He said, "What if he cannot?" He said, "He should help someone troubled by need." He said, "What if he cannot do that?" He said, "He should command what is right or what is good." He said, "What if he does not do that?" He said, "He should refrain from evil. That is *ṣadaqah* for him." (Bukhārī, Muslim)

163. Abū Mūsā ﷺ said, "When someone in need came to the Prophet ﷺ he turned to those sitting with him and said, 'Intercede on behalf of others (for help) and you will be rewarded. Allah accomplishes what He likes through the tongue of His Prophet.' " (Bukhārī, Muslim)

164. Abū Hurayrah ﷺ reported that the Messenger of Allah ﷺ said, "Anyone who calls people to guidance has the same reward as that received by those who follow it, without that decreasing their

reward in any way. Anyone who calls people to misguidance, will have a wrong action like those who follow it, without it decreasing their wrong actions in any way." (Muslim)

165. Abū Hurayrah ؓ reported that the Prophet ﷺ said, "The believer is the believer's mirror and the believer is the believer's brother who guards him against loss and protects him when he is absent." (Abū Dāwūd)

166. Abū Hurayrah ؓ reported that the Messenger of Allah ﷺ said, "Each of you is his brother's mirror. If he sees harm in him, he should remove it from him." (Tirmidhī)

167. Abu'd-Dardā' ؓ reported that the Messenger of Allah ﷺ said, "If anyone defends his brother's honour, Allah will protect his face from the Fire on the Day of Rising." (Tirmidhī)

168. Abū Dharr ؓ reported that the Messenger of Allah ﷺ said, "Your smile to your brother is a *ṣadaqah* for you. Your commanding the correct and forbidding the wrong is a *ṣadaqah*. Your guiding a man in the land of misguidance is *ṣadaqah* for you. Your seeing (showing the way) for a man with bad eyesight is a *ṣadaqah* for you. Your removing a stone or thorn or bone from the road is a *ṣadaqah* for you. Your emptying your bucket (of water) into your brother's (empty) bucket is *ṣadaqah* for you." (Tirmidhī)

169. Abū Hurayrah ؓ reported that the Messenger of Allah ﷺ said, "When the son of Ādam dies, all his actions cease except for three: a *ṣadaqah jāriyah*,[1] or a knowledge which is benefited from, or a righteous son who makes supplication for him." (Muslim)

170. Abū Mas'ūd al-Badrī ؓ reported that the Messenger of Allah ﷺ said, "Anyone who shows the way to something good has the same reward as the person who does it." (Muslim)

---

1. Charity whose benefit is continuous, like planting a tree to shade people from the sun, digging a well to provide water for people, building a mosque, etc., things of common benefit.

14

PUTTING THINGS RIGHT BETWEEN PEOPLE

Allah, Exalted is He, says, *"In most of their secret talks there is no good; but if one exhorts to a deed of charity or justice or conciliation between men."* (4: 114)

He ﷻ says, *"The Believers are but a single brotherhood, so make peace and reconciliation between your two (contending) brothers."* (49: 10)

He ﷻ says: *"Keep straight the relations between yourselves."* (8: 1)

He ﷻ says, *"And such settlement is best."* (4: 128)

171. Sahl ibn Sa'd as-Sā'idī ﷺ reported that the Messenger of Allah ﷺ heard that there was some disagreement among the Banu 'Amr ibn 'Awf. The Messenger of Allah ﷺ went out with some people to make peace between them. The Messenger of Allah ﷺ was delayed and it became time for the prayer. Bilāl went to Abū Bakr ﷺ and said, "Abū Bakr, the Messenger of Allah ﷺ has been delayed and it is time for the prayer. Can you lead the people?" He said, "Yes, if you wish." (Bukhārī, Muslim)

172. Sahl ibn Sa'd ﷺ said, "The people of Qubā' fought to the point that they were stoning one another. The Messenger of Allah ﷺ was informed about that, and said, 'Let us go and make peace between them.' " (Bukhārī)

173. 'Ā'ishah ﷺ said, "The Messenger of Allah ﷺ heard the sound of people quarrelling at the door with raised voices. One of

them was asking the other to reduce his debt and to show him a little leniency. He said, 'By Allah, I will not do it.' The Messenger of Allah ﷺ went out to them and said, 'Where is the one who swore by Allah that he would not do what is good?' He said, 'It was I, Messenger of Allah. He can have whatever he likes.' " (Bukhārī, Muslim)

174. Abū Hurayrah ؓ reported that the Messenger of Allah ﷺ said, "There is *ṣadaqah* owed by every joint that people have every day on which the sun rises. Putting things right between two people is *ṣadaqah*. Helping a man with his mount and helping him onto it or lifting his baggage onto it is *ṣadaqah*. A good word is *ṣadaqah*. Every step you take to the prayer is *ṣadaqah*. Removing an obstruction from the road is *ṣadaqah*." (Bukhārī, Muslim)

175. Umm Kulthūm bint 'Uqbah ibn Abī Mu'ayṭ ؓ reported that: "I heard the Messenger of Allah ﷺ say, 'Someone who puts things right between people and promotes good or says good cannot be called a liar.' " (Bukhārī, Muslim)

176. Abū Bakrah ؓ said, "I saw the Messenger of Allah ﷺ on the *minbar* with al-Ḥasan ibn 'Alī beside him. He would turn to the people and then turn to him. He was saying, 'This grandson of mine is a *sayyid*. Perhaps Allah will make peace by him between two large parties of Muslims." (Bukhārī)

177. Abu'd-Dardā' ؓ reported that the Messenger of Allah ﷺ said, "Shall I tell you what has a higher degree than fasting, prayer and *ṣadaqah*?" They said, "Yes indeed, Messenger of Allah!" He said, "Putting dissension right. Causing dissension is destructive." (Abū Dāwūd)

178. Ḥudhayfah ؓ reported that the Messenger of Allah ﷺ said, "A slanderer will not enter the Garden." (Bukhārī, Muslim)

179. Ibn 'Abbās ؓ reported that the Messenger of Allah ﷺ passed by two graves whose inhabitants were being punished and said, "They are not being punished for anything major (to refrain from). Though indeed, it is major. One of them did not guard himself from urine and the other was involved in back-biting." (Bukhārī, Muslim)

15

BEING DUTIFUL TO PARENTS

Allah, Exalted is He, says, *"Thy Lord hath decreed that ye worship none but Him, and that ye be kind to parents. Whether one or both of them attain old age in thy life, say not to them a word of contempt, nor repel them, but address them in terms of honour. And, out of kindness, lower to them the wing of humility, and say, 'My Lord, bestow on them Thy Mercy even as they cherished me in childhood.'"* (17: 23–24)

He ﷻ says, *"And We have enjoined on man (to be good) to his parents: in travail upon travail did his mother bear him, and in years twain was his weaning: (hear the command): 'Show gratitude to Me and to thy parents.'"* (31: 14)

He ﷻ says: *"We have enjoined on man kindness to his parents: in pain did his mother bear him, and in pain did she give him birth."* (46: 15)

180. 'Abdullāh ibn Mas'ūd ؓ said, "I asked the Prophet ﷺ, 'Which action does Allah Almighty love the most?' He said, 'The prayer in its time.' I said, 'Then what?' He said, 'Dutifulness to parents.' I said, 'Then what?' He said, '*Jihād* in the way of Allah.' " (Bukhārī, Muslim)

181. Abū Hurayrah ؓ said, "A man came to the Messenger of Allah ﷺ and said, 'Messenger of Allah, who is the most entitled to the best of my service?' He said, 'Your mother.' He said, 'Then whom?' He said, 'Your mother.' He said, 'Then whom?' He said, 'Your mother.' He said, 'Then whom?' He said, 'Your father.' " (Bukhārī, Muslim)

182. 'Abdullāh ibn 'Amr ibn al-'Āṣ said, "A man came to the Prophet of Allah and said, 'Shall I give you my oath of allegiance based on emigration and *jihād*, seeking a reward from Allah Almighty?' He said, 'Are either of your parents living?' He said, 'Yes, both of them.' He said, 'Do you desire a reward from Allah Almighty?' He replied, 'Yes.' He said, 'Go back to your parents and keep good company with them.' " (Bukhārī, Muslim)

183. Abū Hurayrah reported that the Prophet said, "May his nose be in the dust! Then may his nose be in the dust! Then may his nose be in the dust!" It was asked, "Who, Messenger of Allah?" He said, "Someone whose parents are old, or one of them is old, and who does not enter the Garden!" (Muslim)

184. Abū Hurayrah reported that the Messenger of Allah said, "No child will repay his father unless he finds him enslaved and then buys him and sets him free." (Muslim)

185. 'Abdullāh ibn 'Umar said, "I had a wife whom I loved but whom (my father) 'Umar disliked. He said to me, 'Divorce her,' and I refused. 'Umar went to the Prophet and mentioned that to him and the Prophet said, 'Divorce her.' " (Abū Dāwūd, Tirmidhī)

186. Mālik ibn Rabī'ah as-Sā'idī said, "Once while we were sitting with the Messenger of Allah a man from the Banū Salamah came up and said, 'O Messenger of Allah, is there any devotion to my parents which I can show them after their death?' He said, 'Yes, praying for them, asking forgiveness for them, fulfilling their pledges after them, maintaining ties of kinship which you only have through them, and honouring any friend of theirs." (Abū Dāwūd)

187. Abu'ṭ-Ṭufayl said, "I saw the Messenger of Allah dividing up meat at al-Ji'rānah when a woman came up to the Prophet . He spread out his cloak for her and she sat on it. I said, 'Who is she?' They said, 'This is his foster mother.' " (Abū Dāwūd)

188. 'Umar ibn as-Sā'ib ﷺ reported that he heard that the Messenger of Allah ﷺ was sitting one day when his foster father came to him. He put down part of his garment for him and he sat on it. Then his foster mother came and he put half of his garment out for her on the other side and she sat on it. Then his foster brother came and he got up for him and made him sit beside him. (Abū Dāwūd)

16

BEING DUTIFUL TO THE FRIENDS OF ONE'S PARENTS AND TO RELATIVES

189. 'Abdullāh ibn Dīnār ❀ reported that when Ibn 'Umar ❀ went out to Makkah, he had a donkey on which he would rest when he was weary of riding his camel and he also wore a turban wrapped round his head. One day when he was on that donkey, he passed a bedouin who said, "Are you not the son of so-and-so?" He said, "I am indeed." So he gave him the donkey and said, "Ride this," and he gave him the turban and said, "Wrap this round your head." One of his companions said to him, "May Allah forgive you! You gave this bedouin the donkey which you were resting on and the turban you had wrapped around your head?" He said, "I heard the Messenger of Allah ❀ say, 'The best form of devotion is to establish relations with a man who loved one's father after his death.' The man's father had been a friend of 'Umar ❀." (Muslim)

190. Mālik ibn Rabī'ah as-Sā'idī ❀ said, "Once while we were sitting with the Messenger of Allah ❀ a man from the Banū Salamah came up and said, 'O Messenger of Allah, is there any devotion to my parents which I can show them after their death?' He said, 'Yes, praying for them, asking forgiveness for them, fulfilling their pledges after them, maintaining ties with relations which you only have through them, and honouring any friend of theirs.' " (Abū Dāwūd)

191. 'Ā'ishah said, "I was never jealous towards any of the other wives of the Prophet as I was jealous of Khadījah even though I never saw her. However, he used to mention her often. And often when he sacrificed a sheep, he would cut it into pieces and send them to Khadījah's friends. I would often say to him, 'It is as if there was only Khadījah in the world!' He would say, 'She was such and such (praising her) and I had children from her.' " (Bukhārī, Muslim)

192. 'Ā'ishah also said, "Hālah bint Khuwaylid, the sister of Khadījah, asked the Messenger of Allah for permission to come in and it reminded him of how Khadījah used to ask permission, and that made him very happy so that he said, 'O Allah, Hālah bint Khuwaylid!' " (Bukhārī, Muslim)

193. Anas ibn Mālik said, "I went out with Jarīr ibn 'Abdullāh al-Bajalī on a journey and he tried to serve me so I said to him, 'Do not do that.' He said, 'I saw the *Anṣār* (your people) serving the Messenger of Allah and I promised myself that I would not keep the company of any of them without serving him.' " (Bukhārī, Muslim)

17

MAINTAINING TIES OF KINSHIP

Allah, Exalted is He, says, "*O mankind! reverence your Guardian Lord, Who created you from a single person, created, of like nature, his mate, and from them twain scattered (like seeds) countless men and women. Fear Allah, through Whom ye demand your mutual (rights) and (reverence) the wombs.*" (4: 1)

He ﷻ says: "*Those who join together those things which Allah hath commanded to be joined.*" (13: 21)

194. Abū Hurayrah ؓ reported that the Messenger of Allah ﷺ said, "Allah Almighty created creation and when He finished creating, kinship stood up and said with Allah's permission, 'Is this the place of him who seeks refuge with You from being cut off?' Allah ﷻ said, 'Yes. Would you be pleased if I joined anyone who joined you and cut off anyone who cut you off?' It said, 'Yes.' Allah ﷻ said, 'Then that is for you.' " Then the Messenger of Allah ﷺ said, "If you wish, then recite, '*Then, is it to be expected of you, if ye were put in authority, that ye will do mischief in the land, and break your ties of kith and kin? Such are the men whom Allah has cursed for He has made them deaf and blinded their sight.*' (47: 22–23)" (Bukhārī, Muslim)

195. 'Ā'ishah ؓ reported that the Prophet ﷺ said, "Kinship is suspended from the Throne and says, 'Allah will connect all those who maintain my ties. Allah will sever His connection with all who sever them.' " (Bukhārī, Muslim)

196. Abū Hurayrah ؓ reported that a man said, "Messenger of Allah ﷺ I have some relatives with whom I maintain relations but

they cut me off. I am good to them and they are bad to me. I am forbearing to them and they are impatient towards me." He ﷺ said, "If you are as you have said, then they are bearing the sin of their deeds (lit. you are throwing hot ashes on them). You will continue to have a helper from Allah against them as long as you remain doing that." (Muslim)

197. 'Abdullāh ibn 'Amr ibn al-'Āṣ ﷺ reported that the Prophet ﷺ said, "A person who maintains ties of kinship is not someone who only does so with those who maintain ties with him. A person who maintains ties of kinship is someone who restores them when they have been cut off." (Bukhārī)

198. Abū Ayyūb Khālid ibn Zayd al-Anṣārī ﷺ reported that a man said, "Messenger of Allah, tell me about an action that will bring me into the Garden and keep me far from the Fire?" The Prophet ﷺ said, "Worship Allah and do not associate anything with Him, perform the prayer and pay the *zakāh* and maintain ties of kinship." (Bukhārī, Muslim)

199. 'Amr ibn 'Abasah ﷺ said, "I visited the Prophet ﷺ in Makkah (i.e. at the beginning of his Prophethood), and I said to him, 'Who are you?' He said, 'A Prophet.' I said, 'And what is a Prophet?' He said, 'Allah has sent me.' I said, 'With what?' He said, 'He has sent me with the task of maintaining ties of kinship, breaking idols, proclaiming that Allah is One and not associating anything with Him.' " (Muslim)

200. Maymūnah bint al-Ḥārith ﷺ set a slave-girl free without asking the permission of the Prophet ﷺ. On the day when he came round to her, she said, "Are you aware, Messenger of Allah, that I have freed my slave-girl?" He said, "Did you do so?" She said, "Yes." He said, "If you had given her to your maternal uncles, you would have had a greater reward." (Bukhārī, Muslim)

201. Anas ﷺ reported that the Messenger of Allah ﷺ said, "Anyone who desires the expansion of his provision or to have the best of his life prolonged, should maintain ties of kinship." (Bukhārī, Muslim)

202. 'Abdullāh ibn 'Amr ibn al-'Āṣ ﷺ said, "I heard the Messenger of Allah ﷺ say openly and not secretly, 'The family of Abū so-and-so are not my supporters. My supporters are Allah and the virtuous believers. However, they do have kinship with me and I will be dutiful to them.' " (Bukhārī, Muslim)

203. Zaynab ath-Thaqafiyyah, the wife of 'Abdullāh ibn Mas'ūd ﷺ said, "The Messenger of Allah ﷺ said, 'Give alms, O congregation of women, even from your jewelry.' " She said, "I went back to 'Abdullāh ibn Mas'ūd and said to him, 'You are a man of little wealth and the Messenger of Allah ﷺ has commanded us to give *ṣadaqah*. So go to him and ask him if [my supporting you] will be enough for me. If not, I will pay it to someone other than you.' He said, 'Rather you should go to him yourself.' So I went and there was one of the women of the *Anṣār* at the door of the Messenger of Allah ﷺ whose situation was similar to mine. The Messenger of Allah ﷺ inspired awe and Bilāl came out to us, so we said to him, 'Go to the Messenger of Allah and tell him that there are two women at the door who are asking him whether *ṣadaqah* to their husbands and the orphans in their care will be enough for them. Do not tell him who we are.' So Bilāl went in to the Messenger of Allah ﷺ and asked him. The Messenger of Allah ﷺ said, 'Who are they?' He said, 'A woman of the *Anṣār* and Zaynab.' The Messenger of Allah ﷺ said, 'Which Zaynab is it?' He said, 'The wife of 'Abdullāh (ibn Mas'ūd).' He said, 'They will both have two rewards: the reward of kinship and the reward of *ṣadaqah*.' " (Bukhārī, Muslim)

204. Anas ibn Mālik ﷺ said, "Abū Ṭalḥah ﷺ had more property in palm trees than any of the *Anṣār* in Madīnah. His favourite property was Bayruḥā' which was opposite the mosque. The Messenger of Allah ﷺ used to enter it and drink its sweet water." Anas said, "When this verse was revealed: *'By no means shall ye attain righteousness unless ye give freely of that which ye love,'* (3: 92) Abū Ṭalḥah went to the Messenger of Allah ﷺ and said, 'Messenger of Allah, Allah Almighty says, *"By no means shall ye attain righteousness unless ye give freely of that which ye love."* The property I love the best is Bayruḥā'.

It is *ṣadaqah* for Allah whose goodness I hope for and I hope that it will be stored up for me with Allah Almighty. Messenger of Allah, dispose of it in whatever way Allah shows you is best.' The Messenger of Allah ﷺ said, 'Excellent! That is a profitable property. That is a profitable property. I have heard what you have said and I think that you should give it to your relatives.' Abū Ṭalḥah said, 'I will do that, Messenger of Allah!' So Abū Ṭalḥah divided it among his relatives and cousins." (Bukhārī, Muslim)

205. Salmān ibn 'Āmir ؓ reported that the Prophet ﷺ said, "*Ṣadaqah* given to a poor person is one *ṣadaqah* but to a relative it is two, both a *ṣadaqah* and maintaining ties of kinship." (Tirmidhī)

18

SPENDING ON DEPENDANTS

Allah, Exalted is He, says, *"They ask thee how much they are to spend. Say: 'What is beyond your needs.'"* (2: 219)

He ﷻ says: *"Let the man of means spend according to his means; and the man whose resources are restricted, let him spend according to what Allah has given him. Allah puts no burden on any person beyond what He has given him."* (65: 7)

He ﷻ says: *"Do ye spend in the least (in His Cause) but He replaces it."* (34: 39)

206. Abū Mas'ūd al-Badrī ﷺ reported that the Prophet ﷺ said, "When a Muslim spends on his family and sincerely hopes to be rewarded for it, it is *ṣadaqah*." (Bukhārī, Muslim)

207. Sa'd ibn Abī Waqqāṣ ﷺ reported that the Messenger of Allah ﷺ said, "It is better to leave heirs rich than to leave them poor, begging from other people. There is nothing you spend, desiring by it the face of Allah, without your being rewarded for it, even a morsel you put in your wife's mouth." (Bukhārī, Muslim)

208. Umm Salamah ﷺ said, "I said, 'Messenger of Allah, will I have a reward if I spend on the children of Abū Salamah and I cannot leave them like this uncared for, when they are also my children?' He ﷺ said, 'Yes, you will have a reward for whatever you spend on them.' " (Bukhārī, Muslim)

209. Abū Hurayrah ﷺ reported that the Messenger of Allah ﷺ said, "Out of a *dīnār* which you spend in the way of Allah and a *dīnār* which you spend on freeing a slave and a *dīnār* which you give to a poor person and a *dīnār* which you spend on your family, the one with the greatest reward is the one which you spend on your family." (Muslim)

210. Thawbān ﷺ, the *mawlā* of the Messenger of Allah ﷺ reported that the Messenger of Allah ﷺ said, "The best *dīnār* a man spends is the *dīnār* which he spends on his family and the *dīnār* which he spends on his mount in the way of Allah and the *dīnār* which he spends on his companions in the way of Allah." (Muslim)

211. 'Abdullāh ibn 'Amr ibn al-'Āṣ ﷺ reported that the Messenger of Allah ﷺ said, "It is enough of a wrong for a man that he neglects someone whom he is supposed to feed." (Abū Dāwūd)

212. Abū Hurayrah ﷺ reported that the Messenger of Allah ﷺ said, "Give *ṣadaqah*!" A man said, "O Messenger of Allah, I have a *dīnār*." He said, "Spend it as *ṣadaqah* on yourself." He said, "I have another." He said, "Give it as *ṣadaqah* to your child." He said, "I have another." He said, "Give it as *ṣadaqah* to your servant." He said, "I have another." He said, "Then you know (better where to spend) it." (Abū Dāwūd, an-Nasā'ī)

213. Harithah ﷺ said, "A man of the Banū 'Udhrah made a resolve to free a slave after he died. The Messenger of Allah ﷺ heard about it and said, 'Do you have any other property?' He said, 'No.' He said, 'Who will buy him from me?' So Nu'aym ibn 'Abdullāh al-'Adawī bought him for eight hundred *dirham*. He brought them to the Messenger of Allah ﷺ who gave them to him. Then he said, 'Begin with yourself and give yourself *ṣadaqah*. If there is anything left over, it is for your family. If there is anything left over from your family, then it is for your relatives. If there is

anything left over from your relatives, then it is like that and like that, (indicating to spend on who is in front of you, to your right and to your left)." (Muslim)

214. 'Umar ibn al-Khaṭṭāb ﷺ reported that the Prophet ﷺ used to sell the fruits of the palm trees of the Banū Naḍīr and would set aside enough food for his family for the year. (Bukhārī)[1]

1. In a variant of Bukhārī, 'Abdullāh ibn 'Umar ﷺ said that the Prophet ﷺ employed the Jews of Khaybar to work the land in return for half of its produce of fruits or other crops. He used to give his wives a hundred *wasq* each, eighty *wasq* of dates and twenty of barley. A *wasq* is sixty *sa'* and in metric weight it is approximately 190 kg.

19

THE RIGHTS OF A HUSBAND ON HIS WIFE

Allah, Exalted is He, says, *"Men are the protectors and maintainers of women, because Allah has given the one more (strength) than the other, and because they support them from their means."* (4: 34)

215. Abū Hurayrah ﷺ reported that the Messenger of Allah ﷺ said, "It is not lawful for a woman to fast while her husband is present, except with his permission, nor to give someone permission to enter his house without his permission." (Bukhārī, Muslim, the wording being that of Bukhārī)

216. Abū Hurayrah ﷺ reported that the Messenger of Allah ﷺ said, "If a man calls his wife to bed and she refuses, causing him to spend the night angry with her, the angels curse her until morning." (Bukhārī, Muslim)

217. 'Abdullāh ibn 'Abbās ﷺ said that the Messenger of Allah ﷺ said, "I was shown the Fire and most of its inhabitants were women who were ungrateful." He was asked, "Were they ungrateful to Allah?" He replied, "They were ungrateful to their husbands and ungrateful for good treatment received. Even if you were always to be good to one of them and then she saw something (else) from you, she would say, 'I have never had anything good from you at all!' " (Bukhārī)

218. Umm Salamah ﷺ reported that the Messenger of Allah ﷺ said, "Any woman who dies at a time when her husband is pleased with her will enter the Garden." (Tirmidhī)

219. Abū Hurayrah ﷺ reported that the Prophet ﷺ said, "If I were to command anyone to prostrate to anyone else, I would have commanded women to prostrate to their husbands." (Tirmidhī)

220. Abū Hurayrah ﷺ also said, "The Messenger of Allah ﷺ was asked, 'Which woman is the best?' He said, 'The one who gives her husband joy when he looks, obeys him when he commands, and does not oppose him in herself and his property with anything he dislikes." (an-Nasā'ī)

221. Usāmah ibn Zayd ﷺ reported that the Prophet ﷺ said, "I have not left after me any trial more harmful to men than women." (Bukhārī, Muslim)

222. Huṣayn ibn Miḥṣan ﷺ reported that an aunt of his went to the Prophet ﷺ and he said to her, "Do you have a husband?" She said, "Yes." He said, "Where do you stand with him?" She said, "I only fall short in that of which I am incapable." He said, "How are you to him? For he is your Garden and your Fire." (an-Nasā'ī)

223. 'Abdullāh ibn 'Amr ibn al-'Āṣ ﷺ reported that the Messenger of Allah ﷺ said, "Allah will not look at a woman who is not grateful to her husband when she cannot dispense with him." (an-Nasā'ī)

20

TREATING WOMEN WELL

Allah, Exalted is He, says, *"Live with them on a footing of kindness and equity."* (4: 19)

He ﷻ says: *"They are your garments and ye are their garments."* (2: 187)

He ﷻ says: *"Ye are never able to be fair and just as between women, even if it is your ardent desire, but turn not away (from a woman) altogether, so as to leave her (as it were) hanging (in the air)."* (4: 129)

224. Abū Hurayrah ؓ reported that the Messenger of Allah ﷺ said, "Hold fast to my admonishment about women, be good to them. Woman was created from a rib. The most crooked part of the rib is the top part. If you try to straighten it, you will break it. If you leave it, it remains crooked. So treat women well." (Bukhārī, Muslim)

225. 'Abdullāh ibn 'Amr ibn al-'Āṣ ؓ reported that the Messenger of Allah ﷺ said, "This world is enjoyment, and the best of its enjoyment is a right acting woman." (Muslim)

226. 'Abdullāh ibn 'Amr ibn al-'Āṣ ؓ also reported that the Messenger of Allah ﷺ said, " 'Abdullāh, have I not been informed that you fast all day and pray all night?" I said, "Yes, Messenger of Allah." He said, "Do not do it. Fast and break the fast, sleep and pray. Your body has a right over you, and your wife has a right over you." (Bukhārī)

227. Abū Hurayrah ؓ reported that the Messenger of Allah ﷺ said, "A believing man should not hate a believing woman. If he

dislikes something in her character, he should be pleased with some other trait of hers." (Muslim)

228. 'Abdullāh ibn Zam'ah said that the Prophet said, "None of you should go and flog his wife as a slave is flogged and then sleep with her at the end of the day." (Bukhārī)

229. Abū Hurayrah reported that the Messenger of Allah said, "Anyone who has two wives and is not equitable between them will come on the Day of Rising with one shoulder lower than the other as if he were falling down." (Tirmidhī)

230. 'Ā'ishah reported that the Messenger of Allah used to say, "O Allah, this is my portion in respect of what I own (have control of). Do not blame me for what You own and I do not own," meaning the heart. (Abū Dāwūd, Tirmidhī and others)

231. Mu'āwiyah ibn Ḥaidah said, "I said, 'Messenger of Allah, what is the right of someone's wife over him?' He said, 'That you feed her when you eat and clothe her when you clothe yourself and do not strike her face. Do not malign her and do not keep apart from her, except within the house.' " (Abū Dāwūd)

232. Abū Hurayrah reported that the Messenger of Allah said, "The most perfect of believers in belief is the best of them in character. The best of you are those who are the best to their women." (Tirmidhī)

233. 'Amr ibn al-Aḥwaṣ al-Jushamī reported that he heard the Prophet say during the Farewell Ḥajj, "You have rights over your women and your women have rights over you. Your right over them is that they do not let anyone you dislike sit on your couches and do not permit those you dislike to enter your house. Their right over you is that you are good to them in respect of their clothes and food." (Tirmidhī)

234. 'Ā'ishah said, "The Abyssinians were playing with their spears and the Messenger of Allah acted as a screen for me

while I was looking. I continued to look until I decided to leave. So estimate how much a young girl is eager for amusement." (Bukhārī)

235. 'Ā'ishah ﷺ reported that the Messenger of Allah ﷺ said, "The best of you are those who are the best to their families, and I am the best to my family." (Ibn Mājah)

236. 'Ā'ishah ﷺ said, "The Messenger of Allah ﷺ raced me and I beat him." (Abū Dāwūd, Ibn Mājah)

237. 'Ā'ishah ﷺ said, "I used to play with other girls in the house of the Prophet ﷺ. Some friends of mine were playing with me when the Messenger of Allah ﷺ came in. They withdrew from him but he sent them back to me to play with me." (Bukhārī, Muslim)

21

TEACHING CHILDREN

Allah, Exalted is He, says, *"O ye who believe! Save yourselves and your families from a Fire."* (66: 6)

He ﷺ says: Allah Almighty says, *"Enjoin prayer on thy people and be constant therein."* (20: 132)

238. 'Abdullāh ibn 'Umar ﷺ said, "I heard the Messenger of Allah ﷺ say, 'All of you are shepherds and each of you is responsible for his flock. An *Imām* (ruler) is a shepherd and he is responsible for those in his care. A man is a shepherd in respect of his family and is responsible for those in his care. The woman is a shepherd in respect of her husband's house and is responsible for those in her care. The servant is a shepherd in respect of his master's property and is responsible for what is in his care. All of you are shepherds and each of you is responsible for his flock." (Bukhārī, Muslim)

239. Abū Hurayrah ﷺ said, "Al-Ḥasan ibn 'Alī ﷺ took a date from the *ṣadaqah* dates and put it in his mouth. The Messenger of Allah ﷺ said, 'No, no! Spit it out'. He said, 'Are you not aware that we do not eat *ṣadaqah*?' " (Bukhārī, Muslim)

240. 'Umar ibn Abī Salamah ﷺ said, "I was a child under the guardianship of the Messenger of Allah ﷺ and my hand would wander around in the dish. The Messenger of Allah ﷺ said to me, 'Boy, say the Name of Allah Almighty and eat with your right hand and eat what is in front of you (close to you).' That became the way I ate ever afterwards." (Bukhārī, Muslim)

241. 'Abdullāh ibn 'Amr ibn al-'Āṣ said that the Messenger of Allah said, "Command your children to pray when they are seven. Beat them (if they fail to do it) when they are ten and separate them in their beds." (Abū Dāwūd)

242. Jābir ibn Samurah reported that the Messenger of Allah said, "It is better for man to teach his child than to give a *sa'* in *ṣadaqah*." (Tirmidhī)

243. Ayyūb ibn Mūsā reported from his grandfather that the Prophet said, "A parent cannot give his child a better gift than good manners (*'ādāb*)." (Tirmidhī)

244. Ibn 'Abbās reported that the Messenger of Allah said, "Anyone who has a daughter and does not bury her alive or prefer his son over her will enter the Garden." (Abū Dāwūd)

245. Anas ibn Mālik reported that the Messenger of Allah said, "I and anyone who brings up two girls until they come of age will be (close) like these two on the Day of Rising," and he put his fingers together. (Muslim)

246. Abū Sa'īd al-Khudrī reported that the Messenger of Allah said, "Anyone who looks after three daughters and instructs them and gives them in marriage and is good to them will be rewarded with the Garden." (Abū Dāwūd)

247. Surāqah ibn Mālik reported that the Messenger of Allah said, "Shall I direct you to the best *ṣadaqah*? When your daughter is returned to you and has no means of support but you." (Ibn Mājah)

248. An-Nu'mān ibn Bashīr reported that his father brought him to the Messenger of Allah and said, "I have given this son of mine a slave that I had." The Messenger of Allah said, "Did you do the same for all your children?" He said, "No." He said, "Fear Allah and be equitable with your children!" So my father came back and that *ṣadaqah* was returned. (Bukhārī, Muslim)

22

KIND TREATMENT OF THE WEAK[1]

Allah, Exalted is He, says, *"And keep thy soul content with those who call on their Lord morning and evening, seeking His Face, and let not thine eyes pass beyond them, seeking the pomp and glitter of this life."* (18: 28)

He ﷻ says: *"And come not nigh to the orphan's property, except to improve it, until he attains the age of full strength."* (6: 152)

He ﷻ says: *"Therefore treat not the orphan with harshness, nor repulse him who asks."* (93: 9–10)

249. Sa'd ibn Abī Waqqāṣ ؓ said, "We were once with the Prophet ﷺ in a group of six. The idol-worshippers said to the Prophet ﷺ, 'Send these men away so that they do not become impudent towards us.' I was there, along with Ibn Mas'ūd, a man from the tribe of Hudhayl, Bilāl and two other men I will not name. There occurred within the soul of the Messenger of Allah ﷺ whatever Allah wished to occur and he thought to himself. So Allah, Exalted is He, sent down, *'Send not away those who call on their Lord morning and evening, seeking His face.'* (6: 52)" (Muslim)

250. 'Ā'idh ibn 'Amr al-Muzanī ؓ reported that Abū Sufyān (leader of the Quraysh before becoming a Muslim) came to Salmān, Ṣuhayb and Bilāl in a group and they said, "The swords of Allah have not finished off the enemy of Allah!" Abū Bakr ؓ said, "Do

---

1. Orphans, widows, daughters, poor people, those who lose heart because of their situation and people in all kinds of difficulties.

you say this to a *shaykh* and leader of the Quraysh?" The Prophet ﷺ came and said, "O Abū Bakr, perhaps you have made them angry? If you were to make them angry, then you would make your Lord angry." He went to them and said, "Brothers, have I made you angry?" They said, "No, may Allah forgive you, brother." (Muslim)

251. Mus'ab ibn Sa'd ibn Abī Waqqāṣ said, "Sa'd thought that he had preference over those beneath him and the Prophet ﷺ said, 'Are you given victory and provision except on account of the weak among you?' " (Bukhārī)

252. Abu'd-Dardā' said, "I heard the Messenger of Allah ﷺ say, 'Find me among the weak. You are only helped (by Allah) and provided for on account of the weak among you." (Abū Dāwūd)

253. Abū Hurayrah reported that the Prophet ﷺ said, "Someone who strives on behalf of widows and the poor is like someone who fights in the way of Allah." I think that he also said, "And like someone who continually stands at night in prayer and like someone who continually fasts." (Bukhārī, Muslim)

254. Abū Hurayrah said that the Prophet ﷺ said, "The worst food is the food of a wedding feast which is denied to those who come to it and which those who are invited refuse to attend.[2] Anyone who does not respond to an invitation has rebelled against Allah and His Messenger." (Muslim)

255. Sahl ibn Sa'd reported that the Messenger of Allah ﷺ said, "I and those who care for orphans will be in the Garden like this," and he pointed with his forefinger and middle finger and made an opening between them. (Bukhārī)

256. Anas ibn Mālik reported that the Messenger of Allah ﷺ said, "I and anyone who brings up two girls until they come of

2. "Those who come to it", i.e. the poor, and "those who are invited and refuse to attend", meaning the rich.

age will be like these two on the Day of Rising," and he put his fingers together. (Muslim)

257. 'Ā'ishah &#x;&#x; said, "A woman came to me with her two daughters to beg and I had nothing but a date which I gave to her. She divided it between her two daughters without eating any of it herself. Then she got up and left. The Prophet &#x;&#x; came to us and I told him about this and he said, 'Anyone who is tried in any way on account of his daughters and is kind to them will find them to be a shield for him from the Fire.' " (Bukhārī, Muslim)

23

THE RIGHTS OF A NEIGHBOUR AND TAKING CARE OF HIM

Allah, Exalted is He, says, *"Serve Allah, and do not associate any partners with Him, and do good – to parents, kinsfolk, orphans, those in need, neighbours who are near, neighbours who are strangers, the companion by your side, the wayfarer (ye meet), and what your right hands possess."* (4: 36)

258. ʿAbdullāh ibn ʿUmar and ʿĀʾishah 🙵 said, "The Messenger of Allah (🙵) said, 'Jibril, peace be upon him, continued to advise me to be good to my neighbour until I thought that he would have me appoint him as my heir.' " (Bukhārī, Muslim)

259. Abū Hurayrah 🙵 reported that the Prophet (🙵) said, "By Allah, he does not believe! By Allah, he does not believe! By Allah, he does not believe!" It was asked, "Who is that, Messenger of Allah?" He said, "Someone whose neighbour is not safe from his mischief!" (Bukhārī, Muslim)

260. Abū Hurayrah 🙵 said that the Messenger of Allah (🙵) said, "O Muslim women! No one should look down on a gift from her neighbour, even if it is only a sheep's trotter." (Bukhārī, Muslim)

261. Abū Hurayrah 🙵 said that the Messenger of Allah (🙵) said, "Anyone who believes in Allah and the Last Day should not harm his neighbour." (Bukhārī, Muslim)

262. Abū Hurayrah ﷺ said that the Messenger of Allah ﷺ said, "No one should prevent his neighbour from inserting a piece of wood in his wall." Then Abū Hurayrah said, "Why is it that you are averse to this? By Allah, I will hurl it at you between your shoulders!" (Bukhārī, Muslim)

263. 'Ā'ishah ﷺ said, "I said, 'Messenger of Allah, I have two neighbours. To which of them should I give?' He said, 'To the one whose door is nearer to you.' " (Bukhārī)

264. Abū Dharr ﷺ reported that the Messenger of Allah ﷺ said, "O Abū Dharr, if you cook a stew put more water in it, keeping your neighbours in mind." (Muslim)

265. 'Abdullāh ibn 'Amr ibn al-'Āṣ ﷺ reported that the Messenger of Allah ﷺ said, "The best of companions in the sight of Allah, is the one who acts best towards his companion. The best of neighbours in the sight of Allah is the one who acts best towards his neighbour." (Tirmidhī)

266. Jābir ibn 'Abdullāh ﷺ said "The Messenger of Allah ﷺ gave a judgement that there should be the right of pre-emption in every partnership, whether in respect of a dwelling or a garden. It is not lawful for one partner to sell his share without informing the other. If he wishes, he can take it, and if he wishes, he can leave it. If one of them sells his share without informing the other, the other has the right to claim it." (Muslim)

267. 'Amr ibn ash-Sharīd said, "Al-Miswar ibn Makhramah ﷺ came and put his hand on my shoulder and I went with him to his maternal uncle Sa'd (ibn Abī Waqqāṣ) ﷺ. Abū Rāfi' ﷺ, (the *mawlā* of the Prophet ﷺ) said to al-Miswar, 'Will you not order this man to buy from me my room which is in his house?' He said,

'By Allah, I will not pay more than four hundred, either in one lump sum or in instalments.' He said, 'I have been offered five hundred cash and I refused them. If it were not that I heard the Prophet ﷺ say, "A neighbour is more entitled by reason of his proximity," I would not give them to you for four hundred.' "[1] (Bukhārī)

1. This *ḥadīth* indicates that because a neighbour has more right to buy the adjacent property, it follows that he also has a right to a more favourable deal. Abū Rāfi' agreed to sell to Sa'd for less than what others had offered him because of his right as a close neighbour, a right which Allah has commanded should be observed, as is stated in the commentary of al-Kirmānī on Bukhārī.

24

HONOURING THE GUEST

Allah, Exalted is He, says, *"Has the story reached thee, of the honoured guests of Abraham? Behold, they entered his presence, and said, 'Peace!' He said, 'Peace!' (And thought, 'These seem) unusual people.' Then he turned quickly to his household, brought out a fatted calf."* (51: 24–26)

He ﷺ says: *"And his people came rushing towards him, and they had been long in the habit of practising abominations. He said: 'O my people! Here are my daughters: they are purer for you (if ye marry)! Now fear Allah, and cover me not with shame about my guests! Is there not among you a single right-minded man?'"* (11: 78)

268. Abū Hurayrah ﷺ reported that the Messenger of Allah ﷺ said, "Anyone who believes in Allah and the Last Day should honour his guest." (Bukhārī, Muslim)

269. Khuwaylid ibn 'Amr (Abū Shurayh al-Ka'bī) ﷺ said, "I heard the Messenger of Allah ﷺ say, 'Anyone who believes in Allah and the Last Day should honour his guest as is his due.' They said, 'What is his due, Messenger of Allah?' He said, 'Kindness and courtesy for a day and a night. Hospitality is for three days, and what is beyond that is *ṣadaqah* for him. It is not lawful for a Muslim to stay with his brother so long that he inconveniences him.' " (Bukhārī, Muslim)

270. Abū Hurayrah ﷺ said, "A man came to the Prophet ﷺ who said, 'Who will give hospitality tonight?' A man of the *Anṣār* said, 'I will, Messenger of Allah.' He took him to his place and said to his wife, 'Do you have anything?' She said, 'No, only the children's

food.' He said, 'Divert them with something else. When they want supper, put them to sleep. When our guest comes in, put out the lamp and we will pretend that we are eating.' So they sat down and the guest ate and they spent the night hungry. In the morning, He went to the Prophet ﷺ and he said, 'Allah was pleased with what you did with your guest last night.' " (Bukhārī, Muslim)

271. Abū Sa'īd al-Khudrī said, "Once when we were on a journey with the Prophet ﷺ a man came on a camel of his and began to look to his right and left. The Messenger of Allah ﷺ said, 'Anyone who has a spare mount should prepare it for someone who does not have a mount to ride, and anyone who has extra provision should prepare it for someone who does not have any provision,' and he mentioned the different categories of property until we thought that none of us had any right to keep anything in excess of our needs." (Muslim)

272. Al-Miqdām ibn Ma'dīkarib reported that the Messenger of Allah ﷺ said, "It is a duty for every Muslim to provide hospitality for a guest for the night. If he is deprived of it, it is a debt he is owed. If he wishes, he can take it, and if he wishes, he can leave it." (Abū Dāwūd)

273. Al-Miqdām also said, "If any man asks people for hospitality and does not receive it, it is a duty for every Muslim to help him, taking the hospitality due to him from his own crops and property." (Abū Dāwūd)

25

COMPASSION TO THE CREATURES OF ALLAH ﷻ IN ONE'S CARE

274. Jarīr ibn 'Abdullāh ؓ reported that the Messenger of Allah ﷺ said, "If someone does not show mercy to other people, Allah will not show mercy to him." (Bukhārī, Muslim)

275. 'Abdullāh ibn 'Amr ibn al-'Āṣ ؓ said, "I heard the Messenger of Allah ﷺ say, 'The All-Merciful shows mercy to those who show mercy. Show mercy to those in the earth and He who is in Heaven will show mercy to you.' " (Abū Dāwūd)

276. Abū Hurayrah ؓ said, "I heard the Messenger of Allah ﷺ say, 'Only the wretched are deprived of mercy.' " (Abū Dāwūd)

277. Abū Hurayrah ؓ reported that the Messenger of Allah ﷺ said, "Anyone who does not show mercy will not have mercy shown to him.' " (Bukhārī, Muslim)

278. Abū Mas'ūd al-Badrī ؓ said, "I was beating a slave with a whip when I heard a voice behind me saying, 'Know, Abū Mas'ūd...' I did not recognise the voice due to my anger. Then, when he drew near me, there was the Messenger of Allah ﷺ and he was saying, 'Know, Abū Mas'ūd, surely Allah the Exalted, has more power over you than you have over this boy.' I said, 'I will never beat a slave after this.' " (Muslim, Abū Dāwūd and others)

279. Zadhān al-Kindī said, "I went to Ibn 'Umar ﵁ when he had freed a slave of his. He picked up a twig or something from the ground and said, 'I will have no reward for it except this. I heard the Messenger of Allah ﷺ say, "If anyone slaps a slave of his, or beats him, his expiation is to set him free." ' " (Muslim and Abū Dāwūd)

280. The steward of Ibn 'Amr ﵁ came to him and he said to him, "Have you given the slaves their food?" He said, "No." So he went and gave it to them, and he said, "The Prophet ﷺ said, 'It is enough wrong action for a man to withhold food from the one he owns.' " (Muslim)

281. 'Abdullāh ibn 'Umar ﵁ said, "A man went to the Prophet ﷺ and said, 'Messenger of Allah, how often should I pardon a servant!' He said, 'Seventy times a day.' " (Abū Dāwūd, Tirmidhī)

282. Hishām ibn Ḥakīm ibn Ḥizām ﵁ said that in Syria he passed by some of the Nabatean peasants who had been made to stand in the sun with oil poured on their heads. He said, "What is this?" He was told, "They are being punished on account of non-payment of land-tax." He said, "I heard the Messenger of Allah ﷺ say, 'Allah will punish those who torture people in this world.' " He went to the *amir* and told him and he commanded that they be released. (Muslim, Abū Dāwūd and an-Nasā'ī)

26

MERCY TO ANIMALS

Allah, Exalted is He, says, *"And before Solomon were marshalled his hosts – of jinns and men and birds, and they were all kept in order and ranks. At length, when they came to a (lowly) valley of ants, one of the ants said: 'O ye ants, get into your habitations lest Solomon and his hosts crush you (under foot) without knowing it."* (27: 17–18)

283. Abū Hurayrah ☙ reported that the Prophet ﷺ said, "Once a man was travelling on a road and became very thirsty. He came across a well, climbed down into it and drank. When he got back out, he found a dog there, panting, which had been driven by thirst to eat mud. He said, 'This dog has reached the same state I was in.' So he climbed back down into the well and filled his leather sock with water and let the dog drink. Allah thanked him for that and forgave him." They said, "Messenger of Allah, do we get a reward then on account of animals?" He said, "There is a reward on account of every live animal [lit. everything with a moist liver]." (Bukhārī, Muslim)

284. Anas ibn Mālik ☙ reported that the Prophet ﷺ said, "There is no Muslim who plants a seedling or sows a crop from which birds, or man or beast then eat without that counting as *ṣadaqah* for him." (Bukhārī)

285. 'Abdullāh ibn 'Umar ☙ reported that the Messenger of Allah ﷺ said, "A woman was punished on account of a cat which she did not feed nor give anything to drink nor allow to eat the earth's rodents and insects." (Muslim)

286. Ibn 'Umar ﵄ reported that he passed by lads from the Quraysh who had set up a bird and were shooting at it, giving the arrow which missed to the owner of the bird as a bet. When they saw Ibn 'Umar, they ran off. Ibn 'Umar said, "Who did this? May Allah curse whoever did this. The Messenger of Allah ﷺ cursed people who used live creatures as targets." (Bukhārī, Muslim)

287. Anas ibn Mālik ﷛ said, "The Messenger of Allah ﷺ forbade tying up animals so that they could be shot at and killed." (Bukhārī, Muslim)

288. Hishām ibn Ḥakim ibn Ḥizām ﷛ reported that a donkey which had been branded on its face passed by the Prophet ﷺ. He said, "May Allah curse whoever branded it." (Muslim)

289. Ibn Mas'ūd ﷛ said, "We were with the Messenger of Allah ﷺ on a journey and he went to relieve himself. We saw a red bird with two chicks and took the chicks. The red bird came up and began to flap its wings. The Prophet ﷺ came back and said, 'Who has distressed this bird by taking its young? Return her young to her.' He saw an ant hill which we had set alight. He said, 'Who has set fire to this?' We replied, 'We did.' He said, 'Only the Lord of the Fire should punish with fire.' " (Abū Dāwūd)

290. 'Abdullāh ibn Jā'far ﵄ said, "He entered a garden belonging to one of the *Anṣār*. There was a camel there. When it saw the Messenger of Allah ﷺ it made a noise and its eyes started watering. The Prophet ﷺ came to it and stroked its back – i.e. its hump and behind its ears – and then it calmed down. He said, 'Who is the owner of this camel? To whom does this camel belong?' A boy of the *Anṣār* came and said, 'It is mine, Messenger of Allah.' He said, 'Do you not fear Allah regarding this dumb animal over which Allah has given you power? It complains to me that you starve it and tire it out.' " (Aḥmad ibn Ḥanbal, Abū Dāwūd)

291. Sahl ibn 'Amr, or as it is said Sahl ibn ar-Rabī' ibn 'Amr ﷛ said, "The Messenger of Allah ﷺ passed by a camel whose back

was sticking to its belly and said, 'Fear Allah in respect of these dumb animals. Ride them in good condition and eat them in good condition.' " (Abū Dāwūd)

292. Abū Hurayrah reported that the Messenger of Allah ﷺ said, "When you travel at a time of fertility, then give the camel its share of the land. When you travel at an arid time, then travel quickly on it and hurry before its hump disappears. When you camp at night, avoid the roadway. Roads are the paths of animals and the refuge of reptiles at night." (Muslim)

27

GOOD MANNERS (*'ĀDĀB*)

Allah, Exalted is He, says, *"O ye who believe! Enter not houses other than your own, until ye have asked permission and saluted those in them."* (24: 27)

He ﷻ says: *"But when the children among you come of age, let them (also) ask for permission, as do those senior to them (in age)."* (24: 59)

He ﷻ says: *"But if ye enter houses, salute each other – a greeting of blessing and purity as from Allah."* (24: 61)

He ﷻ says: *"When a (courteous) greeting is offered you, meet it with a greeting still more courteous, or (at least) of equal courtesy."* (4: 86)

He ﷻ says: *"Eat and drink, but waste not by excess, for Allah loveth not the wasters."* (7: 31)

He ﷻ says: *"O ye Children of Adam! We have bestowed raiment upon you to cover your shame, as well as to be an adornment to you."* (7: 26)

He ﷻ says: *"He made you garments to protect you from heat, and coats of mail to protect you from your (mutual) violence."* (16: 81)

He ﷻ says: *"And made the night as a covering, and made the day as a means of subsistence?"* (78: 10–11)

He ﷻ says: *"Disperse through the land, and seek of the bounty of Allah."* (62: 10)

293. 'Abdullāh ibn 'Amr ibn al-'Āṣ ؓ reported that a man asked the Messenger of Allah (ﷺ), "Which aspect of Islam is best?" He said,

"Feeding people and greeting those you know and those you do not know." (Bukhārī, Muslim)

294. Abū Hurayrah ﷺ reported that the Messenger of Allah ﷺ said, "Someone riding should greet someone walking, and someone walking should greet someone sitting, and a small group should greet a larger group." (Bukhārī, Muslim)

295. Abū Hurayrah ﷺ reported that the Messenger of Allah ﷺ said, "When any of you meets his brother, he should greet him. If a tree or a wall or a stone comes between them and then he again meets him, he should greet him again." (Abū Dāwūd)

296. Abū Dharr ﷺ said, "The Messenger of Allah ﷺ said to me, 'Do not think little of anything which is right, even meeting your brother with a cheerful face.' " (Muslim)

297. Al-Barā' ibn 'Āzib ﷺ reported that the Messenger of Allah ﷺ said, "No two Muslims meet and shake hands without being forgiven before they part." (Abū Dāwūd)

298. 'Ā'ishah ﷺ said, "Zayd ibn Ḥārithah arrived in Madinah when the Messenger of Allah ﷺ was in my room. He came to him and knocked on the door. The Prophet ﷺ was undressed and went to him pulling on his robe and embraced and kissed him." (Tirmidhī)

299. Abū Mūsā al-Ash'arī ﷺ reported that the Messenger of Allah ﷺ said, "You should ask permission to enter three times. If you are given permission, you may enter, if not, you should go away." (Bukhārī, Muslim)

300. Ibn 'Umar ﷺ reported that the Messenger of Allah ﷺ said, "None of you should make a man get up from his place and then sit in it, rather you should make space and make room." When a man got up from his place for Ibn 'Umar, he would not sit there. (Bukhārī)

301. Abū Hurayrah ﷺ reported that the Messenger of Allah ﷺ said, "When one of you gets up from his place and then returns to it, he is more entitled to it." (Muslim)

302. Jābir ibn Samurah ﷺ said, "When we used to come to the Prophet ﷺ we would sit at the edge of the gathering." (Abū Dāwūd, Tirmidhī)

303. 'Abdullāh ibn 'Amr ibn al-'Āṣ ﷺ reported that the Messenger of Allah ﷺ said, "It is not permitted for a man to pass between two people without their permission." (Abū Dāwūd, Tirmidhī)

304. Ibn Mas'ūd ﷺ reported that the Messenger of Allah ﷺ said, "When you are three people together, two should not speak together privately apart from the third until you come together with other people because that might upset him." (Bukhārī, Muslim)

305. Abū Hurayrah ﷺ reported that the Messenger of Allah ﷺ said, "When one of you sneezes, he should say, 'Praise be to Allah,' and his brother or companion should say to him, 'May Allah have mercy on you.' Then he should say, 'May Allah guide you and put your affairs in order.' " (Bukhārī)

306. Thawbān ﷺ reported that the Messenger of Allah ﷺ said, "When a Muslim visits his brother Muslim, he is among the *khurfah* of the Garden until he returns." They said, "Messenger of Allah, what are the *khurfah* of the Garden?" He said, "Its fruits." (Muslim)

307. Ibn 'Abbās ﷺ reported that the Prophet ﷺ went to visit a bedouin who was ill. When he visited him, he said, "No harm. It is a purification if Allah wills." (Bukhārī)

308. 'Ā'ishah ﷺ said, "The Messenger of Allah ﷺ liked to begin with the right in all things – in purification, combing his hair and putting on his shoes." (Bukhārī, Muslim)

309. 'Ā'ishah reported that the Messenger of Allah ﷺ said, "When one of you eats, he should mention the name of Allah Almighty. If he forgets to mention the name of Allah Almighty at the beginning, he should say, 'In the name of Allah, the first of it and the last of it.' " (Abū Dāwūd, Tirmidhī)

310. Abū Hurayrah said, "The Messenger of Allah ﷺ never criticised food. If he liked it, he ate it, and if he disliked it, he left it." (Bukhārī, Muslim)

311. 'Umar ibn Abī Salamah said, "I was a boy in the care of the Messenger of Allah ﷺ and my hand used to go all around in the plate. The Messenger of Allah ﷺ said to me, 'Boy, say the name of Allah, eat with your right hand and eat from what is in front of you.' " (Bukhārī, Muslim)

312. Ibn 'Abbās reported that the Messenger of Allah ﷺ said, "Do not drink all at one go like the camel, rather drink taking two or three breaths. Say the name of Allah when you drink and praise Him when you finish." (Tirmidhī)

313. Anas ibn Mālik reported that the Prophet ﷺ forbade people to drink while standing. Qatādah said, "We said to Anas, 'And eating?' He said, 'That is worse and more offensive.' " (Muslim)

314. Ḥudhayfah said, "The Prophet ﷺ forbade silk and silk brocade, and drinking from gold and silver vessels." He said, "They are for them (non-believers) in this world and they are for you in the Next world." (Bukhārī, Muslim)

315. Ibn 'Abbās related that the Messenger of Allah ﷺ said, "Wear white clothes. They are among the best clothes you have, and shroud your dead in white." (Abū Dāwūd, Tirmidhī)

316. Al-Barā' ibn 'Āzib said, "The Messenger of Allah ﷺ was of medium height. I saw him wearing a red (striped) robe and I have never seen anyone more good looking than him." (Bukhārī, Muslim)

317. Rifā'ah at-Tamīmī ﷺ said, "I saw the Messenger of Allah ﷺ wearing two green garments." (Abū Dāwūd, Tirmidhī)

318. Jābir ﷺ reported that the Messenger of Allah ﷺ entered Makkah on the Day of the Conquest wearing a black turban. (Muslim)

319. 'Ā'ishah ﷺ said, "The Messenger of Allah ﷺ went out one morning wearing a cloak woven from black hair." (Muslim)

320. Ibn 'Umar ﷺ said, "On the Day of Rising Allah will not look at anyone who drags his garment out of arrogance." Abū Bakr ﷺ said, "My wrapper drags if I do not pay attention to it." The Messenger of Allah ﷺ said to him, "You are not one of those who do it out of pride." (Bukhārī)

321. 'Abdullāh ibn 'Amr ibn al-'Āṣ ﷺ reported that the Messenger of Allah ﷺ said, "Allah loves the token of His blessing to be seen on His slaves." (Tirmidhī)

322. Abū Mūsā al-Ash'arī ﷺ reported that the Messenger of Allah ﷺ said, "Wearing silk and gold has been forbidden to the men of my community but is lawful for its females." (Tirmidhī)

323. Anas ibn Mālik ﷺ said, "The Messenger of Allah ﷺ made an exception in the case of az-Zubayr ﷺ and 'Abdurraḥmān ibn 'Awf ﷺ with respect to the wearing of silk in Makkah because of the itchiness they had." (Bukhārī, Muslim)

324. Ka'b ibn Mālik ﷺ said, "The Prophet ﷺ left on the expedition of Tabūk on a Thursday. He liked to set out on Thursdays." (Bukhārī, Muslim)

325. Ibn 'Umar ﷺ reported that the Prophet ﷺ said, "If people knew what I know about travelling alone, no one would travel for a single night alone." (Bukhārī)

326. Abū Saʻīd and Abū Hurayrah ♦ reported that the Messenger of Allah ♦ said, "When three set out on a journey, they should appoint one of them as *amir*." (Abū Dāwūd)

327. Abū Hurayrah ♦ reported that the Messenger of Allah ♦ said, "It is not lawful for a woman who believes in Allah and the Last Day to travel the distance of a day and a night without having a *dhū maḥram* (male relative whom she may not marry) with her." (Bukhārī, Muslim)

328. Abū Hurayrah ♦ said that the Messenger of Allah ♦ said, "Travelling is a form of torment. It deprives a person of his food and drink and sleep. When he fulfils the purpose of his journey, he should hurry back to his family." (Bukhārī, Muslim)

329. Jābir ♦ reported that the Messenger of Allah ♦ said, "When one of you is absent for a long time, he should not return to his family at night (suddenly without informing them)." (Bukhārī, Muslim)

330. Kaʻb ibn Mālik ♦ reported that when the Messenger of Allah ♦ came back from a journey he would first go to the mosque and pray two *rak'ah*. (Bukhārī, Muslim)

331. Abū Hurayrah ♦ reported that the Messenger of Allah ♦ said, "Look to those who are lower than you and do not look to those who are above you. It is more likely that you will not undervalue Allah's blessing to you." (Bukhārī, Muslim)

332. Abū Saʻīd al-Khudrī ♦ reported that the Messenger of Allah ♦ said, "Beware of sitting in the roadways." They said, "Messenger of Allah, we must have places where we can sit and talk together." The Messenger of Allah ♦ said, "If you must sit there, then give the roadway its rights." They asked, "What are the rights of the roadway, Messenger of Allah?" He said, "Lowering the eye, refraining from causing annoyance, returning the greeting, commanding the right and forbidding the wrong." (Bukhārī, Muslim)

333. Abū Sa'īd ﷺ reported that the Messenger of Allah ﷺ said, "A man should not look at another man's private parts nor a woman at another woman's private parts. Two men should not lie naked under the same cover nor two women under the same cover." (Muslim)

334. 'Uqbah ibn 'Āmir ﷺ reported that the Messenger of Allah ﷺ said, "Beware of entering on women!" A man of the *Anṣār* said, "What do you think about in-laws?" He said, "In-laws are death!" (Bukhārī, Muslim)

335. Jābir ﷺ reported that the Prophet ﷺ said, "When a woman comes forward, she comes forward in the form of a Shayṭān. When one of you sees a woman he admires, he should go to his wife. She has the like of what the other one has." (Tirmidhī)

28

ON KEEPING THE BEST COMPANY

Allah, Exalted is He, says, *"Behold, Moses said to his attendant, 'I will not give up until I reach the junction of the two seas or until I spend years and years in travel.' "* (18: 60)

He ﷻ says: *"And keep thy soul content with those who call on their Lord morning and evening, seeking His face."* (18: 28)

336. Abū Mūsā al-Ash'arī ؓ reported that the Messenger of Allah ﷺ said, "The metaphor of a good companion and a bad companion is that of someone with musk and the bellows of the blacksmith. The person with musk either gives it to you, or you buy it or smell its scent, while the bellows of the blacksmith burn your clothes or you get a foul smell from it." (Bukhārī, Muslim)

337. Anas ibn Mālik ؓ reported that the Messenger of Allah ﷺ said, "The metaphor of a good companion is that of someone with musk. Even if you do not actually get any of it, you still get its scent. The metaphor of a bad companion is that of someone with bellows. Even if the soot from them does not get to you, the smoke does." (Abū Dāwūd, an-Nasā'ī)

338. Abū Hurayrah ؓ reported that the Messenger of Allah ﷺ said, "People are like mines of gold and silver. The best of them in the *Jāhiliyyah* is the best of them in Islam if they have understanding. The spirits are gathered in ranks like troops. Those which knew one another are in harmony. Those which did not know one another are discordant." (Muslim)

339. Abū Hurayrah 🙵 also reported that the Prophet 🙵 said, "A man follows the way of life of his close friend, so each of you should be very careful about whom he takes as a close friend." (Abū Dāwūd, Tirmidhī)

340. Abū Saʿīd al-Khudrī 🙵 reported that the Prophet 🙵 said, "Take only a believer as a friend and let only someone Godfearing eat your food." (Abū Dāwūd, Tirmidhī)

341. Abū Idrīs al-Khawlānī said, "I entered the mosque of Damascus and there was a young man with shining (white) teeth sitting with some people. When they disagreed about something, they referred it to him and followed his opinion. I inquired about him and it was said, 'That is Muʿādh ibn Jabal.' The following day, I went early and I found that he had come earlier than me and I found him praying. I waited for him until he finished his prayer and then I approached him from the front. I greeted him and then said, 'By Allah, I love you for Allah.' He said, 'By Allah?' I said, 'By Allah.' He said, 'By Allah?' I said, 'By Allah.' He took hold of the upper part of my cloak and pulled me to him. He said, 'Rejoice! I heard the Messenger of Allah 🙵 say, "Allah Almighty says, 'My love is mandatory for those who love one another in Me and sit together for My sake and who visit one another for My sake and who give generously to one another for My sake.' " ' " (Mālik transmitted it in al-Muwaṭṭāʾ)

342. Thawbān 🙵 said, "When it was revealed, 'And there are those who treasure up gold and silver,' (9: 34), we were with the Messenger of Allah 🙵 on one of his journeys. One of his Companions said, 'It was sent down about gold and silver. If we knew any wealth which was better, we would take it.' He said, 'The best wealth is a tongue which remembers (Allah), a grateful heart and a believing wife who helps one in belief.' " (Tirmidhī)

343. Abū Hurayrah 🙵 reported that the Prophet 🙵 said, "A woman can be married for four reasons: her wealth, her lineage, her beauty, and her religion. Attain the one with religion. May your hands be in the dust!" (Bukhārī, Muslim)

29

ON GOOD CHARACTER AND HUMBLENESS

Allah, Exalted is He, says, *"And thou (standest) on an exalted standard of character."* (68: 4)

He ﷻ says: *"Who restrain anger, and pardon (all) men, for Allah loves those who do good."* (3: 134)

He ﷻ says: *"And swell not thy cheek (for pride) at men, nor walk in insolence through the earth: For Allah loveth not any arrogant boaster."* (31: 18)

344. Anas ibn Mālik ﷺ said, "The Messenger of Allah ﷺ had the best character of all people." He said, "I did not touch any brocade or silk softer than the palm of the Messenger of Allah ﷺ. I did not smell any scent sweeter than the scent of the Messenger of Allah. I served the Messenger of Allah ﷺ for ten years and he never said, 'Uff' to me, nor did he remark about anything I had done, 'Why did you do that?' nor about anything I had not done, 'Why did you not do that?' " (Bukhārī, Muslim)

345. Anas ibn Mālik ﷺ said, "If one of the slave-girls of Madinah took the hand of the Prophet ﷺ, she could take him wherever she liked." (Bukhārī)

346. Anas ibn Mālik ﷺ passed by some children and greeted them, saying, "The Messenger of Allah ﷺ used to do that." (Bukhārī, Muslim)

347. An-Nawwās ibn Sam'ān ﷺ said, "I asked the Messenger of Allah ﷺ about piety and wrong action. He said, 'Piety is good character and wrong action is what troubles your heart and you hate other people to discover." (Muslim)

348. 'Abdullāh ibn 'Amr ibn al-'Āṣ ﷺ said, "The Messenger of Allah ﷺ was neither obscene nor indecent. He used to say, 'The best of you are those who are the best in character." (Bukhārī, Muslim)

349. Abu'd-Dardā' ﷺ reported that the Messenger of Allah ﷺ said, "There will be nothing heavier in the balance of the believer on the Day of Rising than good character. Allah hates foul language." (Tirmidhī)

350. Abū Hurayrah ﷺ said, "The Messenger of Allah ﷺ was asked about the things most likely to bring people into the Garden. He said, '*Taqwā* of Allah and good character.' He was asked about the things most likely to bring people into the Fire. He said, 'The mouth and the genitals.' " (Tirmidhī)

351. Abū Hurayrah ﷺ said that the Messenger of Allah ﷺ said, "The believers with the most perfect belief are the best of them in character. The best of you are those of you who are best towards your wives." (Tirmidhī)

352. 'Ā'ishah ﷺ said, "I heard the Messenger of Allah ﷺ say, 'By his good character a believer can reach the same rank as someone who fasts and prays at night." (Abū Dāwūd)

353. Abū Umāmah al-Bāhilī ﷺ reported that the Messenger of Allah ﷺ said, "I guarantee a house on the outskirts of the Garden to anyone who abstains from arguing, even when he is in the right, and a house in the middle of the Garden for anyone who abandons lying, even when he jests, and a house at the summit of the Garden for anyone who has good character." (Abū Dāwūd)

354. Jābir reported that the Messenger of Allah said, "Those I love most and those sitting nearest to me on the Day of Rising will be those of you with the best character. Those most hateful to me and the furthest of you from me on the Day of Rising will be the pompous, the braggarts and the arrogant.' They said, 'Messenger of Allah, we know the pompous and the braggarts, but who are the arrogant?' He said, 'The proud.' " (Tirmidhī)

355. 'Iyaḍ ibn Ḥimār reported that the Messenger of Allah said, "Allah revealed to me that you should be humble towards each other. So no one should vaunt himself above another and no one should commit injustice against another." (Muslim)

356. Abū Hurayrah reported that the Messenger of Allah said, "*Ṣadaqah* does not decrease property; Allah only increases a slave in might by forgiveness; and no one is humble for the sake of Allah without Allah elevating him." (Muslim)

30

ON FORBEARANCE, PATIENCE AND KINDNESS

Allah, Exalted is He, says: *"Hold to forgiveness; command what is right, but turn away from the ignorant."* (7: 199)

He ﷻ says: *"Let them forgive and overlook, do you not wish that Allah should forgive you?"* (24: 22)

He ﷻ says: *"Nor can Goodness and Evil be equal. Repel (Evil) with what is better: Then will he between whom and thee was hatred become as it were thy friend and intimate. And no one will be granted such goodness except those who exercise patience and self-restraint – none but persons of the greatest good fortune."* (41: 34–35)

He ﷻ says: *"But indeed if any show patience and forgive, that would truly be an exercise of courageous will and resolution in the conduct of affairs."* (42: 43)

357. 'Ā'ishah ﵂ said, "The Messenger of Allah ﷺ was never given a choice between two matters without taking the easier of them, as long as it was not a sin. If it was a sin, he was the furthest of people from it. The Messenger of Allah ﷺ never took revenge himself for anything unless it violated the sanctity of Allah. Then he would take revenge for the sake of Allah, Exalted is He." (Bukhārī, Muslim)

358. 'Ā'ishah ﵂ also said, "The Messenger of Allah ﷺ never struck anyone with his hand, including women and servants, unless he was fighting in the way of Allah. He did not demand retaliation for anything that happened to him, unless one of the sacred things of

Allah was violated, then he would retaliate only for the sake of Allah, Exalted is He." (Muslim)

359. Anas ﷺ said, "I was walking with the Messenger of Allah ﷺ and he was wearing a Najrāni cloak with a thick border. A bedouin came up to him and pulled the cloak violently. I looked at the Prophet's shoulder, and it had been marked by the border of the cloak due to the severity of his pull. Then he said, 'Muḥammad! Allot me some of the property of Allah which you have.' He turned to him and laughed and then ordered a gift to be given to him." (Bukhārī, Muslim)

360. Abū Hurayrah ﷺ said, "A bedouin urinated in the mosque. The people moved towards him (to fall on him) and the Prophet ﷺ said, 'Leave him and pour a bucket or pail of water onto his urine. You were sent to make things easy and not to make them difficult.' " (Bukhārī)

361. Ibn 'Abbās ﷺ reported that the Messenger of Allah ﷺ said to Ashajj 'Abdu'l-Qays ﷺ, "You have two qualities which Allah and His Messenger love: forbearance and steadiness." (Muslim)

362. Ibn Mas'ūd ﷺ said, "It is as if I could see the Messenger of Allah ﷺ recounting that the people of one of the Prophets, struck and wounded him, and he said as he wiped the blood from his face, 'O Allah, forgive my people because they do not know.' " (Bukhārī, Muslim)

363. 'Ā'ishah ﷺ reported that the Messenger of Allah ﷺ said, "Allah is kind and loves kindness and gives for gentleness what he does not give for harshness or anything else." (Muslim)

364. 'Ā'ishah ﷺ also said, "Whenever kindness is in a thing it adorns it, and whenever it is removed from anything, it disfigures it." (Muslim)

365. Shaddād ibn Aws ﷺ reported that the Messenger of Allah ﷺ said, "Allah has decreed kindness for everything. So when you

kill,[1] kill well. When you slaughter,[2] slaughter well. Each of you should sharpen the edge of his knife and should calm his animal." (Muslim)

366. Abū Hurayrah ﷺ reported that the Messenger of Allah ﷺ said, "The strong man is not the one who throws people in wrestling. The strong man is the one who has control of himself when he is angry." (Bukhārī, Muslim)

367. Abu'd-Dardā' ﷺ reported that the Prophet ﷺ said, "Whoever is given his share of kindness has been given his share of good. Whoever is denied his share of kindness has been denied his share of good." (Tirmidhī)

368. Ibn Mas'ūd ﷺ reported that the Messenger of Allah ﷺ said, "Shall I inform you about the one for whom the fire is forbidden? It is the one who draws near to the people, is easy going and gentle." (Tirmidhī)

369. Ibn 'Abbās ﷺ said about the words of Allah, Exalted is He, *"Repel evil with that which is best,"* (23: 96), "Patience in anger and pardon for evil-doing. When they act, Allah will protect them and humble their enemy to them in their presence." (Bukhārī mentioned this *ḥadīth* with partial *isnād*.)

1–2. Meaning to use the sharpest tool which will inflict the least pain.

31

ON TRUSTWORTHINESS AND FULFILLING CONTRACTS

Allah, Exalted is He, says: *"O ye who believe! Betray not the trust of Allah and the Messenger, nor misappropriate knowingly things entrusted to you."* (8: 27)

He ﷻ says: *"Allah doth command you to render back your trusts to those to whom they are due."* (4: 58)

He ﷻ says: *"Fulfil (every) promise, for (every) promise will be enquired into (on the Day of Rising)."* (17: 34)

He ﷻ says: *"Fulfil the Covenant of Allah when ye have entered into it."* (16: 91)

He ﷻ says: *"O ye who believe! Fulfil (all) obligations."* (5: 1)

He ﷻ says: *"Why say ye that which ye do not? Grievously odious is it in the sight of Allah that ye say that which ye do not."* (61: 2–3)

370. Abū Hurayrah ﷺ reported that the Messenger of Allah ﷺ said, "There are three signs of a hypocrite: whenever he speaks, he lies; whenever he makes a promise, he breaks it; and whenever he is trusted, he betrays his trust." (Bukhārī, Muslim)

371. 'Abdullāh ibn 'Amr ibn al-'Āṣ ﷺ reported that the Messenger of Allah ﷺ said, "If anyone has four characteristics, he is a pure hypocrite, and if anyone has one of them, he has an aspect of hypocrisy until he gives it up: whenever he is trusted, he betrays his trust; whenever he speaks, he lies; whenever he makes an

agreement, he breaks it; and whenever he quarrels, he deviates from the truth, speaking falsely." (Bukhārī, Muslim)

372. Ḥudhayfah ؈ said, "The Messenger of Allah ﷺ related two aḥādīth to us. I have seen one of them (come true) and am still waiting for the other. He related to us that trustworthiness had descended into the hearts of men. Then the Qur'ān descended and they learnt from the Qur'ān and they learnt from the *Sunnah*. Then he related to us about the removal of trustworthiness, and he said, 'A man will go to sleep and trustworthiness will be taken from his heart and its trace will remain like a small mark. Then he will go to sleep and trustworthiness will be taken from his heart and its trace will remain like a weal, as when an ember rolls onto his foot and it blisters up and you see it raised up with nothing in it.' Then he took some pebbles and rolled them onto his foot." (Bukhārī, Muslim)

373. Jābir ؈ said, "The Messenger of Allah ﷺ said to me, 'If the money from Baḥrayn comes, I will give you such-and-such.' The money from Baḥrayn did not come until after the Prophet ﷺ had died. When the money of Baḥrayn arrived, Abū Bakr commanded that it be announced, 'Whoever has a promise from the Messenger of Allah ﷺ or a debt should come to us.' I came to him and said, 'The Prophet ﷺ told me such-and-such.' He gave me a double handful and I counted them and there were five hundred. He said, 'Take twice as much again.' " (Bukhārī, Muslim)

374. 'Abdullāh ibn 'Āmir ؈ said, "One day my mother called me when the Messenger of Allah ﷺ was sitting in our house. She said, 'Come, I will give you something.' The Messenger of Allah ﷺ said to her, 'What are you intending to give him?' She said, 'I intend to give him some dates.' The Messenger of Allah ﷺ said to her, 'If you do not give him anything, a lie will be recorded against you.' " (Abū Dāwūd)

375. Zayd ibn Arqam ؈ reported that the Prophet ﷺ said, "If someone makes a promise to his brother with the intention of fulfilling

it and he could not fulfil it or the agreed time of fulfilling the promise did not arrive, he incurs no sin." (Abū Dāwūd, Tirmidhī)

376. Ibn 'Umar said, "The Messenger of Allah ﷺ came to us and said, 'O company of *Muhājirūn*! There are five things by which you may be tested – and I seek refuge with Allah from them reaching you: fornication does not appear amongst people so that they are open about it without the plague spreading among them, as well as diseases which did not occur among their ancestors in the past. They do not give short measure or weight without being afflicted by drought, great trouble and tyranny from their ruler. They do not refuse to pay the *zakāh* due on their cattle without being denied rain from the sky. Were it not for the beasts, they would not have any rain at all. They do not break the contract with Allah and His Messenger without Allah giving their enemy power over them who then takes some of what they possess. When their leaders do not judge by the Book of Allah and choose what Allah has sent down, Allah makes them fight one another." (Ibn Mājah)

32

ON TRUTHFULNESS

Allah, Exalted is He, says, *"O you who believe! Fear Allah and be with those who are true (in word and deed)."* (9: 119)

He ﷻ says: *"It were best for them if they were true to Allah."* (47: 21)

He ﷻ says: *"Not a word does he utter but there is a sentinel near him, ready (to note it)."* (50: 18)

He ﷻ says: *"And pursue not that of which thou hast no knowledge."* (17: 36)

He ﷻ says: *"For (every act of) hearing, or (of) seeing, or of (feeling in) the heart will be enquired into (on the Day of Reckoning)."* (17: 36)

377. Ibn Mas'ūd ﷺ reported that the Prophet ﷺ said, "You must be truthful. Truthfulness leads to dutiful obedience and dutiful obedience leads to the Garden. A man is truthful and seeks truthfulness until he is written down as truthful with Allah. Lying leads to deviance and deviance leads to the Fire. A man lies and seeks falsehood until he is written down as a liar with Allah." (Bukhārī, Muslim)

378. From Abū Sufyān ﷺ, in a long *ḥadīth* concerning what happened with Heraclius, is that he said, "Heraclius said, 'What does he order you to do?' I said, 'He says, "Worship Allah alone and do not associate anything with Him and abandon what your ancestors said. He commands us to pray, to speak the truth, to give *ṣadaqah*, to be chaste, and to maintain ties of kinship.' " (Bukhārī, Muslim)

379. Ḥakīm ibn Ḥizām ﷺ said that the Prophet ﷺ said, "The seller and the buyer have the option (to withdraw) as long as they

have not yet separated. If they speak the truth and make things clear, they will be blessed in their sale. If they conceal things and lie, the blessing of their transaction will be wiped out." (Bukhārī, Muslim)

380. Ibn 'Umar ؓ said that the Prophet ﷺ said, "The worst kind of accusation is that a person attributes to his eyes (of seeing something) which they have not seen." (Bukhārī)

381. Sufyān ibn Usayd al-Ḥaḍramī ؓ said, "I heard the Messenger of Allah ﷺ say, 'It is great treachery on your part to tell your brother something when he believes you and you are lying to him.' " (Abū Dāwūd)

382. Ṣafwān ibn Sulaym ؓ said, "The Prophet ﷺ was asked, 'Messenger of Allah, can a believer be a coward?' He said, 'Yes.' He was asked, 'Can a believer be a miser?' He said, 'Yes.' He was asked, 'Can a believer be a liar?' He said, 'No.' " (Mālik)

383. 'Abdullāh ibn 'Āmir ؓ said, "One day my mother called me when the Messenger of Allah ﷺ was sitting in our house. She said, 'Come, I will give you something.' The Messenger of Allah ﷺ said to her, 'What are you intending to give him?' She said, 'I intend to give him some dates.' The Messenger of Allah ﷺ said to her, 'If you do not give him anything, a lie will be recorded against you.' " (Abū Dāwūd)

384. Bahz ibn Ḥakīm reported that his grandfather said, "I heard the Messenger of Allah ﷺ say, 'Woe to the man who recounts something to make people laugh when he is lying. Woe to him! Woe to him!' " (Abū Dāwūd, Tirmidhī and others)

385. Abū Hurayrah ؓ reported that the Prophet ﷺ said, "It is enough of a lie that a man should recount all that he hears." (Muslim)

386. Al-Ḥasan ibn 'Alī ؓ said, "I memorised from the Messenger of Allah ﷺ, 'Abandon that which gives you doubt for that which gives you no doubt. Truthfulness is peace of mind and lying is doubt.' " (Tirmidhī)

33

ON MODESTY

Allah, Exalted is He, says, *"Afterwards one of the (damsels) came (back) to him, walking bashfully."* (28: 25)

He ﷺ says: *"Such (behaviour) annoys the Prophet. He is ashamed to dismiss you, but Allah is not ashamed (to tell you) the truth."* (33: 53)

387. Ibn 'Umar ☺ reported that the Messenger of Allah ﷺ passed by one of the men of the *Anṣār* who was admonishing his brother for being too modest. The Messenger of Allah ﷺ said, "Let him be. Modesty is part of belief." (Bukhārī, Muslim)

388. 'Imrān ibn al-Ḥuṣayn ☺ reported that the Messenger of Allah ﷺ said, "Modesty only brings good." (Bukhārī, Muslim)

389. Abū Hurayrah ☺ reported that the Messenger of Allah ﷺ said, "Belief has over seventy or over sixty branches. The best of which is the words, 'There is no god but Allah,' and the least of which is removing an obstruction from the road. Modesty is a branch of belief." (Bukhārī, Muslim)

390. Abū Hurayrah ☺ reported that the Messenger of Allah ﷺ said, "Modesty is part of belief, and belief is in the Garden. Vulgarity is part of coarseness and coarseness is in the Fire." (Tirmidhī)

391. Abū Umāmah ☺ reported that the Messenger of Allah ﷺ said, "Modesty and reticence are two branches of belief. Vulgarity and verbosity are part of hypocrisy." (Tirmidhī)

392. Anas ibn Mālik ﷺ reported that the Messenger of Allah ﷺ said, "Whenever there is immodesty in a thing, it disfigures it. Whenever there is modesty in a thing, it adorns it." (Ibn Mājah)

393. From Zayd ibn Ṭalḥah ibn Rukānah ﷺ that the Prophet ﷺ said, "Every *dīn* has an innate character. The character of Islam is modesty." (Mālik)

394. Abū Sa'īd al-Khudrī ﷺ said, "The Messenger of Allah ﷺ was more modest than a virgin in her private room. When he saw something he disliked, we could see it in his face." (Bukhārī, Muslim)

395. Abū Mas'ūd ﷺ reported that the Messenger of Allah ﷺ said, "Part of what has reached people of the words of the earliest Prophethood is: if you do not have shame, then do whatever you like." (Bukhārī)

396. Abū Mas'ūd ﷺ reported that the Messenger of Allah ﷺ said, "Be modest before Allah with a proper measure of modesty." He said, "We said, 'O Prophet of Allah. We are modest, praise be to Allah!' He said, 'That is not what is meant. Proper modesty before Allah is to guard the head and what it contains and the belly and what it contains and to remember death and trial. Whoever desires the Next World should abandon the adornment of this world. Whoever does that has been modest before Allah with a proper measure of modesty.' " (Tirmidhī)

34

ON STEADFASTNESS IN AFFLICTION

Allah, Exalted is He, says, *"Be sure We shall test you with something of fear and hunger, some loss in goods or lives or the fruits (of your toil), but give glad tidings to those who patiently persevere, who say, when afflicted with calamity, 'To Allah we belong and to Him is our return.'"* (2: 155–156)

He ﷻ says: *"Those who patiently persevere will truly receive a reward without measure."* (39: 10)

He ﷻ says: *"But indeed if any show patience and forgive, that would truly be an exercise of courageous will and resolution in the conduct of affairs."* (42: 43)

397. Usāmah ibn Zayd ﷺ said, "A daughter[1] of the Prophet ﷺ sent a message to him, saying, 'One of my sons is dying, so come.' He sent his greetings to her and said, 'What Allah takes is His and what He gives is His. Everything has a fixed term with Him so she should be patient and expect a reward.' She sent to him imploring him to come to her. He got up with Sa'd ibn 'Ubādah and some other Companions ﷺ. The child was brought to the Messenger of Allah and he was shuddering. The Prophet's eyes overflowed with tears and Sa'd said, 'Messenger of Allah, what is this?' He said, 'This is mercy which Allah has put in the hearts of His slaves. Allah is only merciful to those of His slaves who are merciful.' " (Bukhārī, Muslim)

1. This was Zainab the wife of Abul 'Āṣ ﷺ.

398. Anas ibn Mālik said, "The Prophet ﷺ passed by a woman who was weeping at a grave and said, 'Have *taqwā* of Allah and be patient.' She said, not recognising him, 'Leave me alone. You have not been struck by such an affliction as mine!' She was told, 'It is the Prophet ﷺ.' She went to the door of the Prophet ﷺ and, finding no one guarding the door, she said, 'I did not recognise you.' He said, 'The time for patience is only at the first shock.' " (Bukhārī, Muslim)

399. Abū Sa'īd and Abū Hurayrah reported that the Prophet ﷺ said, "No fatigue, illness, anxiety, sorrow, harm or sadness afflicts any Muslim, even as much as a thorn pricking him, without Allah making them as expiation for his sins." (Bukhārī, Muslim)

400. Abū Hurayrah reported that the Prophet ﷺ said, "The metaphor of a believer when he is afflicted by a calamity is that of a fresh tender plant. No matter which direction the wind comes from, it bends, and when the wind stops, it stands straight again. An impious person is like a pine tree which remains rigid and straight until Allah breaks it when He wishes." (Bukhārī)

401. Anas ibn Mālik said, "I heard the Messenger of Allah ﷺ say, 'Allah the Mighty and Exalted says, 'When I test My slave in the two things he loves and he is patient, I repay him for them with the Garden.' " He meant his eyes. (Bukhārī)

402. Ṣuhayb ibn Sinān reported that the Messenger of Allah ﷺ said, "What an extraordinary thing the business of the believer is! All of it is good for him. And that only applies to the believer. If good fortune is his lot, he is grateful and it is good for him. If something harmful happens to him, he is patient and that is good for him too." (Muslim)

403. Anas ibn Mālik reported that the Messenger of Allah ﷺ said, "When Allah desires good for one of His slaves, He brings forward the punishment for him in this world. When Allah desires evil for His slave, He withholds from him what is due to him on

account of his wrong action and then settles it on the Day of Rising." The Prophet ﷺ said, "The greatness of the reward is from the greatness of the trial. When Allah, Exalted is He, loves a person, He tests them. Whoever is content has contentment, and whoever is displeased has displeasure." (Tirmidhī)

404. Abū Hurayrah ؓ reported that the Messenger of Allah ﷺ said, "Believers, both men and women, will continue to be tried in respect of themselves, their children and their property until they meet Allah, Exalted is He, without any wrong action at all." (Tirmidhī)

405. Ibn 'Umar ؓ reported that the Messenger of Allah ﷺ said, "A believer who mixes with people and endures their harm is better than a believer who does not mix with people or endure their harm." (Ibn Mājah)

35

ON THANKFULNESS

Allah, Exalted is He, says, *"Then do ye remember Me; I will remember you. Be grateful to Me, and reject not faith."* (2: 152)

He ﷻ says, *"If ye are grateful, I will add more (favours) unto you."* (14: 7)

He ﷻ says: *"And the close of their cry will be, 'Praise be to Allah, the Cherisher and Sustainer of the Worlds.'"* (10: 10)

He ﷻ says, *"But the bounty of thy Lord, rehearse and proclaim!"* (93: 11)

406. Ṣuhayb ibn Sinān ؓ reported that the Messenger of Allah ﷺ said, "What an extraordinary thing the business of the believer is! All of it is good for him. And that only applies to the believer. If good fortune is his lot, he is grateful and it is good for him. If something harmful happens to him, he is patient and that is good for him too." (Muslim)

407. Anas ibn Mālik ؓ reported that the Messenger of Allah ﷺ said, "Allah is pleased with a slave of His who eats something and praises Him for it and drinks something and praises Him for it." (Muslim)

408. Al-Mughīrah ibn Shu'bah ؓ said, "The Messenger of Allah ﷺ used to pray at night until his feet became cracked. He was asked, 'Why do you do this, Messenger of Allah, when Allah has forgiven you all your past and future slips?' He said, 'Should I not be a grateful slave?' " (Tirmidhī)

409. Ibn 'Umar ﷺ reported that the Messenger of Allah ﷺ said, "If anyone asks for refuge by Allah, Allah gives him refuge. If anyone asks by Allah, give to him. If anyone asks for protection by Allah, give him protection. If anyone brings you something correct, recompense him. If you do not find anything (to give him), then make supplication for him until you know that you have compensated him." (Abū Dāwūd, an-Nasā'ī. The wording is of al-Nasā'ī)

410. Anas ibn Mālik ﷺ said, "The *Muhājirūn* said, 'O Messenger of Allah! The *Anṣār* have taken all the reward. We have not seen any people more generous than them when they have a lot, or better at sharing when they have little. They have spared us hardship.' He ﷺ said, 'Do you not praise them and make supplication for them?' They said, 'Yes.' He said, 'Then that is for that (i.e. that is the recompense for that).' " (Abū Dāwūd, an-Nasā'ī)

411. Jābir ibn 'Abdūllah ﷺ reported that the Messenger of Allah ﷺ said, "Anyone who is given a gift and is pleased with it should give something in return. If he does not have anything, he should praise the gift. Whoever praises it has been thankful for it. Whoever conceals it, has been ungrateful for it." (Abū Dāwūd, Tirmidhī)

412. Usāmah ibn Zayd ﷺ reported that the Messenger of Allah ﷺ said, "If anyone has something good done for him, he should say to the person who did it, 'May Allah repay you well.' He has then been ample in his praise." (Tirmidhī)

413. Abū Hurayrah ﷺ reported that the Messenger of Allah ﷺ said, "Anyone who does not thank people does not thank Allah." (Abū Dāwūd, Tirmidhī)

36

ON RELIANCE (ON ALLAH ﷻ)

Allah, Exalted is He, says, *"Believers are those who, when Allah is mentioned, feel a tremor in their hearts, and when they hear His signs rehearsed, find their faith strengthened, and put (all) their trust in their Lord."* (8: 2)

He ﷻ says: *"Then, when you have taken a decision, put your trust in Allah. For Allah loves those who put their trust (in Him)."* (3: 159)

He ﷻ says: *"And put your trust in Him Who lives and dies not."* (25: 58)

He ﷻ says: *"And if anyone puts his trust in Allah, sufficient is (Allah) for him."* (65: 3)

414. Abū Bakr aṣ-Ṣiddīq ؓ said, "I saw the feet of the idol-worshippers when we were in the Cave and the idol-worshippers were right over our heads, and I said, 'Messenger of Allah, if one of them were to look under his feet, he would see us.' He ﷺ said, 'Abū Bakr, what do you think of two people of whom Allah is the Third?' " (Bukhārī, Muslim)

415. Ibn 'Abbās ؓ reported that the Messenger of Allah ﷺ said, "Seventy thousand of my community will enter the Garden without reckoning. They are those who do not make charms (or ask others for charms) or look for omens, and they depend on their Lord." (Bukhārī)

416. Ibn 'Abbās ⚶ said, "*Allah is enough for us and the best Guardian.*" Ibrāhīm, peace be upon him, said this when he was thrown into the Fire and Muḥammad ﷺ said it when they said, "People are gathering against you, so fear them," but it only increased their faith; and they said, "Allah is enough for us and the best Guardian." (3: 173) (Bukhārī)

417. Abū Hurayrah ⚶ reported that the Prophet ﷺ said, "People will enter the Garden whose hearts are like the hearts of birds." (Muslim)

418. 'Umar ibn al-Khaṭṭāb ⚶ said, "I heard the Messenger of Allah ﷺ say, 'If you were to rely on Allah as He should be relied on, He would provide for you as He provides for the birds. They go out in the morning hungry and return in the evening full.' " (Tirmidhī)

419. Anas ibn Mālik ⚶ said, "There were two brothers in the time of the Prophet ﷺ. One of them used to come to the Prophet ﷺ and the other one worked for a living. The one who worked complained about his brother to the Messenger of Allah ﷺ who said, 'It might well be that you have your provision on account of him.' " (Tirmidhī)

37

ON *TAQWĀ*

The basis of *taqwā* is to protect oneself from associating things with Allah ﷻ, then to protect oneself from acts of disobedience and then to protect oneself from doubtful things.

Allah, Exalted is He, says: *"O you who believe, fear Allah as He should be feared and die not except in a state of Islam."* (3: 102)

He ﷻ says: *"So fear Allah as much as you can."* (64: 16)

He ﷻ says: *"If you fear Allah, He will grant you a Criterion (to judge between right and wrong), remove from you (all) evil (that may afflict) you, and forgive you."* (8: 29)

He ﷻ says: *"And for those who fear Allah, He (ever) prepares a way out, and He provides for him from (sources) he could never imagine."* (65: 2, 3)

He ﷻ says: *"The most honoured of you in the sight of Allah is (he who is) the most righteous of you."* (49: 13)

420. Abū Sa'īd al-Khudrī ﷺ reported that the Messenger of Allah ﷺ said, "This world is green and sweet. Allah will put you in charge of it to see how you act. Beware of this world and beware of women, for the first trial experienced by the Children of Israel was on account of women." (Muslim)

421. Abū Dharr and Mu'ādh ibn Jabal ﷺ reported that the Messenger of Allah ﷺ said, "Fear Allah wherever you are and follow up an evil action with a good action which will wipe it out, and treat people well." (Tirmidhī)

422. Abū Hurayrah said, "The Messenger of Allah was asked about the things most likely to bring people into the Fire. He said, 'The mouth and the genitals.' He was asked about the things most likely to bring people into the Garden. He said, '*Taqwā* of Allah and good character.' " (Tirmidhī)

423. An-Nu'mān ibn Bashīr said, "I heard the Messenger of Allah say, 'The *ḥalāl* is clear and the *ḥarām* is clear. But between the two there are doubtful things about which many people have no knowledge. Whoever protects himself from doubtful matters keeps his *dīn* and his honour pure. Whoever gets involved in ambiguities falls into the *ḥarām*. Like a herdsman who grazes his animals near a private preserve (*ḥimā*). He is bound to enter it. Every king has a private preserve and the private preserve of Allah on His earth are the things that He has made forbidden. There is a lump of flesh in the body, which when it is sound, the entire body is sound, and when it is corrupt, the entire body is corrupt – it is the heart.' " (Bukhārī, Muslim)

424. Wābiṣah ibn Ma'bad said, "I came to the Messenger of Allah and he said, 'Have you come to ask about *taqwā*?' I said, 'Yes.' He said, 'Consult your heart. Piety is that with which the self is at rest and the heart is at rest and wrong action is what is closely knit in your self and echoes to and fro in your breast, even if people repreatedly give judgement in your favour.'" (Aḥmad, ad-Dārimī)

425. 'Aṭiyyah ibn 'Urwah reported that the Messenger of Allah said, "The slave will not be one of the people of *taqwā* until he abandons that in which there is no harm as a precaution against that in which there is harm." (Tirmidhī)

426. Al-Ḥasan ibn 'Alī said, "I memorised from the Messenger of Allah, 'Leave what gives you doubt for what gives you no doubt.' " (Tirmidhī)

38

ON PERSEVERANCE IN ACTIONS AND HASTENING TO PERFORM THEM

Allah, Exalted is He, says, *"Has not the time arrived for the believers that their hearts in all humility should engage in the remembrance of Allah and of the Truth which has been revealed (to them), and that they should not become like those to whom was given revelation aforetime, but long ages passed over them and their hearts grew hard?"* (57: 16)

He ﷻ says: *"And be not like a woman who breaks into untwisted strands the yarn she has spun after it has become strong."* (16: 92)

He ﷻ says: *"And serve thy Lord until there come unto thee (the Hour that is) Certain."* (15: 99)

427. 'Ā'ishah ﵂ reported that the Messenger of Allah ﷺ said, "Do good deeds properly, and abandon excess and know that it is not your deeds which will take you into the Garden (but the bounty of Allah) and that the action which Allah loves the most is the one which is most constant, even if it is little." (Bukhārī)

428. 'Alqamah ibn Qays said, "I asked the Umm al-Mu'minīn, 'Ā'ishah ﵂ 'Umm al-Mu'minīn! What were the actions of the Prophet ﷺ like? Did he single out any days?' She said, 'No. His action was regular and constant. Which of you is capable of what the Prophet ﷺ was capable of?' " (Bukhārī)

429. 'Ā'ishah ﵂ said, "When the Messenger of Allah ﷺ missed the (*tahajjud*) prayer in the night due to illness or some other reason, he would pray twelve *rak'ah* during the daytime." (Muslim)

430. 'Umar ibn al-Khaṭṭāb ﷺ said, "Anyone who sleeps through his *ḥizb* (supererogatory prayer or recitation of the Qur'ān) or part of it, should recite it between the *Fajr* prayer and the *Ẓuhr* prayer. It will be written for him as if he had recited it in the night." (Muslim)

431. Abū Hurayrah ﷺ said, "A man came to the Messenger of Allah ﷺ and said, 'Messenger of Allah, which *ṣadaqah* has the greatest reward?' He said, 'That you give *ṣadaqah* while you are healthy yet tight-fisted, fearing poverty and desiring wealth. Do not put it off until death is near and you say, "So-and-so should have this much and so-and-so this much," when it already belongs to someone else.' " (Bukhārī, Muslim)

432. Abū Hurayrah ﷺ reported that the Messenger of Allah ﷺ said, "Race to good actions before seven things. What are you waiting for except delayed poverty, wealth – which leads to extravagance, debilitating illness, doddering senility, sudden death or the *Dajjāl*? And he (the *Dajjāl)* is an evil unseen one to be waited for, or the Last Hour? The Last Hour will be more bitter and terrible." (Tirmidhī)

433. Abū Umayyah ash-Sha'bānī ﷺ said, "I asked Abū Tha'labah al-Khushanī, 'Abū Tha'labah! What do you say about this *āyah*: *"Guard your own selves..."* (5: 105)?' He said, 'By Allah, you have asked an expert about it! I asked the Messenger of Allah ﷺ about it. He said, "Rather enjoin the correct and forbid the incorrect until the time when you see avarice being obeyed, passion being followed, this world being preferred and everyone admiring his own opinion. Then you must guard your own self and leave what the masses are doing. Ahead of you are days requiring patience, and patience in those days will be like grasping live coals. The one who acts in those days will have the reward of fifty men who act as he does." ' " (Abū Dāwūd, Tirmidhī and Ibn Mājah)

39

MODERATION IN OBEDIENCE

Allah, Exalted is He, says: *"Ta-Ha. We have not sent down the Qur'ān to you to be (an occasion) for your distress."* (20: 1–2)

He ﷻ says, *"Allah intends every facility for you; He does not want to put you in difficulties."* (2: 185)

He ﷻ says: *"O People of the Book! Commit no excesses in your religion nor say of Allah aught but the truth."* (4: 171)

He ﷻ says: *"On no soul doth Allah place a burden greater than it can bear."* (2: 286)

434. Abū Juḥayfah Wahb ibn 'Abdullāh ﷺ said, "The Prophet ﷺ joined Salmān and Abu'd-Dardā' ﷺ together in brotherhood. Salmān visited Abu'd-Dardā' and saw Umm ad-Dardā' poorly dressed and said to her, 'What's the matter with you?' She said, 'Your brother Abu'd-Dardā' has no need of this world.' Abu'd-Dardā' came and made some food for him. Salmān said, 'Eat.' He said, 'I am fasting.' Salmān said, 'I will not eat unless you eat.' " He said, "He ate. In the night, Abu'd-Dardā' went to stand in prayer and Salmān said to him, 'Sleep!' and he slept. Then he got up again and Salmān said, 'Sleep!' At the end of the night, Salmān said, 'Now get up and we will pray.' Salmān said to him, 'Your Lord has rights over you, your self has rights over you, and your wife has rights over you so give those with rights their due.' Abu'd-Dardā' came to the Prophet ﷺ and mentioned this to him and the Prophet ﷺ said, 'Salmān spoke the truth.' " (Bukhārī)

435. 'Abdullāh ibn 'Amr ibn al-'Āṣ said, "The Prophet was informed that I had said, 'By Allah, I will fast all day and pray all night for as long as I live.' The Prophet said, 'Did you say that?' I said to him, 'I did say it, may my father and mother be your ransom, Messenger of Allah.' He said, 'You will not be able to do it. So fast and break the fast, and pray and sleep. Fast three days of the month and since every good action is multiplied by ten that will be like fasting all the time.' I said, 'I can do better than that.' He said, 'Then fast one day and break the fast for two days.' I said, 'I can do better than that.' He said, 'Then fast one day and break the fast the next. That is the fast of (Prophet) Dāwūd, peace be upon him, and there is no fast better than that.' Now (later in his old age he said) that I had accepted the three days which the Prophet suggested would have been dearer to me than my family and my property." (Bukhārī, Muslim)

436. Anas ibn Mālik said, "Three people came to the houses of the wives of the Prophet to ask about how the Prophet worshipped. When they were told, it was as if they thought it was little and said, 'Where are we in relation to the Messenger of Allah who has been forgiven his past and future wrong actions?' One of them said, 'As for me, I will pray all night every night.' Another said, 'I will fast all the time and not break the fast.' The other said, 'I will withdraw from women and never marry.' The Messenger of Allah came to them and said, 'Are you the ones who said such-and-such? By Allah, I am the one among you with the most fear and *taqwā* of Allah, but I fast and break the fast, I pray and I sleep, and I marry women. Whoever shuns my *sunnah* is not of me.' " (Bukhārī, Muslim)

437. Ibn 'Abbās said, "Once while the Prophet was speaking (giving the *khuṭbah*), he saw that a man remained standing, and he asked about him. They said, 'It is Abū Isra'il who vowed to stand in the sun without sitting down or seeking shade or speaking and (he vowed) to fast.' The Prophet said, 'Command him to speak, seek shade and sit down but he should complete his fast.' " (Bukhārī)

438. Anas ibn Mālik ☙ said, "The Prophet ❀ entered the mosque and there was a rope hanging between two pillars. He said, 'What is this rope?' They said, 'The rope belongs to Zaynab. When she is tired, she hangs on to it.' The Prophet ❀ said, 'No – remove it. You should pray as long as you have the energy for it. When you are tired, you should sleep.' " (Bukhārī, Muslim)

439. 'Ā'ishah ☙ said that once the Prophet ❀ came when a woman was with her. He asked, "Who is this?" She replied, "So-and-so," and told him about the amount she prayed. He said, "Stop! You must only do what you are able. By Allah, Allah does not grow weary [of giving rewards] until you grow weary, and the dīn He likes best is the one in which there is constancy." (Bukhārī, Muslim)

440. 'Ā'ishah ☙ reported that the Messenger of Allah ❀ said, "When one of you dozes off while he is praying, he should go and lie down until sleepiness leaves him. If someone prays when he is drowsy, he may not know, perhaps he means to ask for forgiveness, but he is abusing himself." (Bukhārī, Muslim)

441. Abū Hurayrah ☙ reported that the Messenger of Allah ❀ said, "The dīn is easy. Anyone who makes the dīn too hard on himself will find that it overpowers him. So aim for what is right, follow a middle path, accept the good news [of the reward for right action] and seek help [to reach your goal by being constant in worshipping] in the morning, evening and some of the night." (Bukhārī)

442. Jābir ibn Samurah ☙ said, "I used to pray the prayers with the Prophet ❀ and his prayer was of medium length and his khuṭbah was of medium length." (Muslim)

443. 'Ā'ishah ☙ reported that the Prophet ❀ said, "What is wrong with certain people who refrain from doing something I do? By Allah, I have the most knowledge of any of them of Allah and am the most fearful of them towards Him." (Bukhārī)

40

ON THE MERIT OF THE QUR'ĀN AND ITS RECITATION

Allah, Exalted is He, says: *"This is the Book; in it is guidance sure, without doubt, to those who fear Allah; who believe in the unseen."* (2: 2–3)

And He ﷻ says: *"(It is) a Qur'ān which We have divided (into parts from time to time), in order that thou mightest recite it to men at intervals: We have revealed it by stages."* (17: 106)

And He ﷻ says: *"Recite the Qur'ān in slow, measured rhythmic tones."* (73: 4)

And He ﷻ says: *"And when they hear His revelations rehearsed, they find their faith strengthened."* (8: 2)

And He ﷻ says: *"Had We sent down this Qur'ān on a mountain, verily thou wouldst have seen it humble itself and cleave asunder for fear of Allah. Such are the similitudes which We propound to men, that they may reflect."* (59: 21)

And He ﷻ says: *"And We have indeed made the Qur'ān easy to understand and remember: then is there any that will receive admonition?"* (54: 17)

444. Abū Umāmah ؓ said, "I heard the Messenger of Allah ﷺ say, 'Recite the Qur'ān. It will come on the Day of Rising as an intercessor for its people.' " (Muslim)

445. 'Ā'ishah ؓ reports that the Messenger of Allah ﷺ said, "The one who recites the Qur'ān fluently, is with the noble pious

angels. And the one who recites the Qur'ān and stammers in it and it is difficult for him has two rewards." (Muslim)

446. Abū Mūsā al-Ash'arī ❀ reported that the Messenger of Allah ❀ said, "The example of the believer who recites the Qur'ān is like that of a citron – its scent is pleasant and its taste is good and the example of the believer who does not recite the Qur'ān is like that of a date – it has no scent but its taste is sweet. The example of a hypocrite who recites the Qur'ān is like that of basil – its scent is nice but its taste is bitter and the example of a hypocrite who does not recite the Qur'ān is like that of a colocynth – it has no scent and its taste is bitter." (Bukhārī, Muslim)

447. Ibn 'Umar ❀ reported that the Prophet ❀ said, "There is no envy except for two things: a man to whom Allah has given the Qur'ān and he recites it during the day and night, and a man to whom Allah has given wealth and he spends it throughout the night and the day." (Bukhārī, Muslim)

448. Ibn Mas'ūd ❀ said, "The Prophet ❀ said to me, 'Recite the Qur'ān to me.' I said, 'Messenger of Allah, shall I recite to you when it was revealed to you?' He said, 'I want to hear it from someone other than myself.' So I recited *Sūrah* an-Nisā' to him until I reached this *āyah*, '*How then if We brought from each people a witness, and We brought thee as a witness against these people?*' (4: 41) He said, 'That is enough now,' and I turned to him and his eyes were flowing with tears." (Bukhārī, Muslim)

449. Abū Hurayrah ❀ reported Allah's Messenger ❀ as saying, "No group of people assemble in one of the houses of Allah (mosques) reciting the Book of Allah and studying it together but without which tranquillity descends upon them, mercy covers them, the angels surround them and Allah mentions them in the presence of those with Him." (Muslim)

450. Abū Sa'īd Rāfi' ibn al-Mu'allā ❀ reported that, "The Messenger of Allah ❀ said to me, 'Shall I teach you the greatest

sūrah of the Qur'ān before you leave the mosque?' and he took my hand. When we were about to leave, I said, 'Messenger of Allah, you said, "I will teach you a *sūrah* of the Qur'ān?" He said, "Praise be to Allah, Lord of the worlds" (the *Fātiḥah*) it is the seven oft-repeated ones and the magnificent Qur'ān which I was given.' " (Bukhārī)

451. Ubayy ibn Ka'b ﷺ said, "The Messenger of Allah ﷺ said, 'Abu'l-Mundhir! Which *āyah* in the Book of Allah is the greatest according to you?' I said, *'Allah! There is no god but He – the Living, the Self-Subsisting, Eternal.'* (*Āyat al-Kursī*, 2: 255) He struck me on the chest and said, 'May knowledge delight you, Abu'l-Mundhir!' " (Muslim)

452. Abū Hurayrah ﷺ narrated: Allah's Messenger ﷺ entrusted me with guarding the *Zakāh* revenue of Ramaḍān. Then somebody came to me and started stealing from the foodstuff. I caught him and said, "I will take you to Allah's Messenger ﷺ!" Then Abū Hurayrah described the whole story: That person said (to me), "When you go to your bed, recite *Āyat al-Kursī* (2: 255) for then there will be a guard from Allah who will protect you all night long, and no shayṭān will be able to come near you till dawn." (When he heard the story) the Prophet ﷺ said (to me), "He (who came to you at night) told you the truth although he is a liar; and that was a shayṭān." (Bukhārī)

453. Abū Mas'ūd al-Badrī ﷺ reported that the Prophet ﷺ said, "If anyone recites the two *āyats* at the end of Sūrah al-Baqarah at night, they will be enough for him (i.e. against any misfortune)." (Bukhārī, Muslim)

454. Abū Hurayrah ﷺ narrated that the Messenger of Allah ﷺ said, "Do not turn your houses into graveyards. Shayṭān flees from any house in which Sūrah al-Baqarah is recited." (Muslim)

455. An-Nawwās ibn Sam'ān ﷺ said, "I heard the Messenger of Allah ﷺ say, 'On the Day of Resurrection the Qur'ān and those who acted according to it will be brought with Sūrah al-Baqarah and Āl 'Imrān preceding it.' The Messenger of Allah ﷺ gave three similes,

which I did not forget afterwards. He (the Prophet) said, 'It is as if they are two clouds, or two black canopies with light between them, or two flocks of birds in ranks pleading for the one who recited them.' " (Muslim)

456. Abū Umāmah al-Bāhilī ؓ said that he heard Allah's Messenger ﷺ say, "Recite the Qur'ān, for on the Day of Resurrection it will come as an intercessor for those who recite it. Recite the two bright ones, al-Baqarah and Āl 'Imrān, for on the Day of Resurrection they will come as two clouds or two shades, or two flocks of birds in ranks, pleading for those who recite them. Recite Sūrah al-Baqarah, for to take it is a blessing and to give it up is a cause of grief, and the magicians cannot confront it." (Muslim)

457. Abu'd-Dardā' ؓ reported Allah's Messenger ﷺ as saying, "If anyone memorises the first ten *āyats* of Sūrah al-Kahf, he will be protected from the *Dajjāl*." (In another narration it is: "From the beginning of Sūrah al-Kahf.") (Muslim)

458. Al-Barā' ibn 'Āzib ؓ said, "A man was reciting Sūrah al-Kahf and he had a horse near him tethered by two ropes. Then a cloud came over him and drew nearer and his horse began to bolt. In the morning he went to the Prophet ﷺ and mentioned that to him and he said, 'That was the *Sakīnah* which descended on account of the Qur'ān.' " (Bukhārī, Muslim)

459. 'Umar ibn al-Khaṭṭāb ؓ reported that Allah's Messenger ﷺ said, "A *sūrah* has been revealed to me tonight which is dearer to me than that over which the sun rises (i.e. the world). Then he recited: *'Verily! We have given you (Muḥammad), a manifest victory.'* " (48: 1) (Bukhārī)

460. Abū Hurayrah reported Allah's Messenger ﷺ as saying, "A *sūrah* in the Qur'ān containing thirty verses interceded for a man till he was forgiven. It was *'Blessed is He in Whose hands is the kingdom'*." (67: 1) (Abū Dāwūd, Tirmidhī)

461. Abū Sa'īd al-Khudrī ﷺ reported that a man heard another man reciting, *"Say: He is Allah, the One and Only,"* (112: 1) repeating it over and over. In the morning he went to the Messenger of Allah ﷺ and mentioned that to him, and it was as if he considered the *sūrah* a trifle. The Messenger of Allah ﷺ said to him, "By the One who has my soul in His hand, it is equal to a third of the Qur'ān." (Bukhārī)

462. 'Uqbah ibn 'Āmir ﷺ reported that the Messenger of Allah ﷺ said, "Have you not seen the *āyats* sent down this night the like of which have never been seen before? *'Say: I seek refuge with the Lord of the Dawn,'* (113: 1) and *'Say: I seek refuge with the Lord and Cherisher of mankind.'* " (114: 1) (Muslim)

463. 'Ā'ishah ﷺ narrated: "Whenever Allah's Messenger ﷺ became sick he would recite the Mu'awwidhāt (Sūrah Al-Falaq and Sūrah An-Nās) and then blow into his hands and rub them over his body. When he became seriously ill I used to recite (these two *Sūrahs*) and rub his hands over his body hoping for its blessings." (Bukhārī)

464. 'Ā'ishah ﷺ narrated: "When the Prophet ﷺ went to bed every night, he used to recite Sūrah Al-Ikhlāṣ, Sūrah Al-Falaq and Sūrah An-Nās, cup his palms together and blow into them; and then rub his hands over whatever parts of his body he was able to rub, starting with his head, face and the front of his body, doing that three times." (Bukhārī)

41

ON INVOCATIONS

Allah, Exalted is He, says: *"Then do ye remember Me; I will remember you. Be grateful to Me, and reject not Faith."* (2: 152)

And He ﷻ says: *"And do thou bring thy Lord to remembrance in thy (very) soul, with humility and remember without loudness in words, in the mornings and evenings; and be not thou of those who are unheedful."* (7: 205)

And He ﷻ says: *"(Lit is such a Light) In houses, which Allah hath permitted to be raised to honour; for celebration, in them, of His name: in them is He glorified. In the mornings and in the evenings, (again and again)."* (24: 36)

And He ﷻ says: *"O ye who believe! Remember Allah, with much remembrance; and glorify Him morning and evening."* (33: 41, 42)

And He ﷻ says: *"O ye who believe! Let not your riches or your children divert you from the remembrance of Allah. If any act thus, surely they are the losers."* (63: 9)

465. Abū Hurayrah ﷺ reported Allah's Messenger ﷺ as stating that Allah says, "I am as My slave thinks of Me, and I am with him when he remembers Me. If he remembers Me within himself I shall remember him within Myself, and if he remembers Me in an assembly I shall remember him in an assembly better than his." (Bukhārī, Muslim)

466. Abū Hurayrah ﷺ reported that Allah's Messenger ﷺ said, "The *mufarridūn* have gone ahead and excelled." They asked, "Who are the *mufarridūn*, Messenger of Allah?" He replied, "Those men and women who remember Allah much." (Muslim)

467. 'Abdullāh ibn Busr ◈ mentioned that a man said, "Messenger of Allah! The ordinances of Islam have become too many for me, so tell me something to which I can cling." He ◈ replied, "Keep your tongue moist with the remembrance of Allah." (Tirmidhī transmitted it, saying, "This is a *ḥasan ḥadīth*.")

468. Jābir ◈ said, "I heard the Messenger of Allah ◈ say, 'The best remembrance is لَا إِلَهَ إِلَّا اللَّهُ *Lā ilāha illallāh – There is no god but Allah.*' " (Tirmidhī)

469. Abū Hurayrah ◈ said, "Allah's Messenger ◈ said, 'Two expressions, [which are] light on the tongue, heavy in the scale and dear to the Compassionate One, are; سُبْحَانَ اللَّهِ وَبِحَمْدِهِ *Subḥāna'l lāhi wa bi ḥamdihī – Glory be to Allah", and* [I begin] *with praise of Him;* and سُبْحَانَ اللَّهِ الْعَظِيمِ *Subḥāna'l lāhi'l 'aẓīm – Glory be to Allah the Incomparably Great*' " (Bukhārī, Muslim)

470. Abū Mūsā al-Ash'arī ◈ said, "The Messenger of Allah ◈ said to me, 'Shall I not guide you to one of the treasures of the Garden?' I said, 'Certainly, Messenger of Allah.' He said, لَا حَوْلَ وَلَا قُوَّةَ إِلَّا بِاللَّهِ *'Lā ḥawla wā lā Quwwata illā billāh – There is no might and no power except by Allah.*' " (Bukhārī, Muslim)

471. Abū Ayyūb al-Anṣārī ◈ reported that the Prophet ◈ said, "Anyone who says,

لَا إِلَهَ إِلَّا اللَّهُ وَحْدَهُ لَا شَرِيكَ لَهُ، لَهُ الْمُلْكُ وَلَهُ الْحَمْدُ يُحْيِي وَيُمِيتُ وَهُوَ عَلَى كُلِّ شَيْءٍ قَدِيرٌ

'Lā ilāha illa'llāhu waḥdahū lā sharīka lahū lahu'l mulku wa lahu'l ḥamdu wa huwa 'alā kulli shay'in qadīr – There is no god but Allah alone without partner. His is the kingdom and His is the praise. He has power over everything' ten times, it is as if he had set free four slaves of the descendants of Ismā'īl." (Bukhārī, Muslim)

472. Juwairiyah bint al-Hārith, the Mother of the Believers ◈ said that the Prophet ◈ went out after morning prayer leaving her sitting in her place of prayer (making *dhikr* and *du'ā'*). He returned in the forenoon and she was still sitting [in the same place]. He asked, "Have you continued in the same

position I left you in?" She said, "Yes." So the Prophet (ﷺ) said, "Since leaving you I have said four phrases three times which, if weighed against all you have said today, would prove to be heavier: سُبْحَانَ اللهِ وَبِحَمْدِهِ ، عَدَدَ خَلْقِهِ ، وَرِضَى نَفْسِهِ ، وَزِنَـــةَ عَرْشِـــهِ ، وَمِدَادَ كَلِمَاتِهِ *'Subḥāna'llāhi 'adada khalqihī wa riḍā nafsihī wa zināta 'arshihī wa midāda kalimātih – Glory be to Allah, as much as the number of His creatures; and, in accordance with His good pleasure; and as much as the weight of His throne; and as much as the extent of His words.'* " (lit: according to the ink of His words.) (Muslim)

473. Abū Hurayrah ؓ reported that the poor emigrants (*Muhājirūn*) came to Allah's Messenger (ﷺ) and said, "The possessors of wealth have obtained all the highest grades and abiding bliss. They pray as we do, they fast as we do, but they have an excess of wealth with which they perform *Ḥajj* and *'Umrah*, go on *jihād* and pay their *zakāh*." So Allah's Messenger (ﷺ) said, "Shall I not teach you something by which you will catch up with those who have preceded you and race ahead of those who come after you, with no-one being better than you except those who do as you do?" They replied, "Certainly, Messenger of Allah." He said, "Glorify [Allah], praise, and declare [His] greatness, thirty-three times after every prayer." (Bukhārī, Muslim)

474. 'Alī ibn Abī Ṭālib ؓ said that Fāṭimah ؓ went to the Prophet (ﷺ) to request from him a servant, but did not find him. So, finding 'Ā'ishah ؓ, she mentioned the matter to her. 'Alī ؓ said, "The Prophet (ﷺ) came to us when we had gone to bed, and said, 'Shall I not point out to you something better than having a servant? When you go to bed, say, سُبْحَانَ اللهِ *"Subḥāna'llāh – Glory be to Allah"* thirty-three times, الْحَمْدُ لله *"Al-ḥamdu li'llāh – Praise be to Allah"* thirty-three times, and اللهُ أَكْبَر *"Allāhu Akbar – Allah is Most Great"* thirty-three times. That will be better for you than a servant.' " (Other narrations mention either 34 *Tasbīḥ* (glorifications) or 34 *takbīrs*.) (Bukhārī, Muslim)

475. Abū Hurayrah ﷺ reported Allah's Messenger ﷺ as saying, "Allah Most High has ninety-nine names, one hundred less one. He who comprehends them will enter Paradise. He is,

اَللّٰهُ الَّذِي لَاۤ إِلَهَ إِلاَّ هُوَ الرَّحْمَنُ الرَّحِيمُ الْمَلِكُ الْقُـــــدُّوسُ السَّـــلَامُ الْمُؤْمِنُ الْمُهَيْمِنُ الْعَزِيزُ الْجَبَّارُ الْمُتَكَبِّرُ الْخَالِقُ الْبَارِئُ الْمُصَوِّرُ الْغَفَّـــارُ الْقَهَّارُ الْوَهَّابُ الرَّزَّاقُ الْفَتَّاحُ الْعَلِيمُ الْقَابِضُ الْبَاسِطُ الْخَافِضُ الرَّافِـعُ الْمُعِزُّ الْمُذِلُّ السَّمِيعُ الْبَصِيرُ الْحَكَمُ الْعَدْلُ اللَّطِيفُ الْخَبِيرُ الْحَلِيمُ الْعَظِيــمُ الْغَفُورُ الشَّكُورُ الْعَلِيُّ الْكَبِيرُ الْحَفِيظُ الْمُقِيتُ الْحَسِيبُ الْجَلِيلُ الْكَـرِيمُ الرَّقِيبُ الْمُجِيبُ الْوَاسِعُ الْحَكِيمُ الْوَدُودُ الْمَجِيدُ الْبَاعِثُ الشَّهِيدُ الْحَـقُّ الْوَكِيلُ الْقَوِيُّ الْمَتِينُ الْوَلِيُّ الْحَمِيدُ الْمُحْصِي الْمُبْدِئُ الْمُعِيدُ الْمُحْيِي الْمُمِيتُ الْحَيُّ الْقَيُّومُ الْوَاجِدُ الْمَاجِدُ الْوَاحِدُ الصَّمَدُ الْقَـــادِرُ الْمُقْتَـــدِرُ الْمُقَدِّمُ الْمُؤَخِّرُ الْأَوَّلُ الْأَخِرُ الظَّاهِرُ الْبَاطِنُ الْوَالِيَ الْمُتَعَالِي الْبَرُّ التَّوَّابُ الْمُنْتَقِمُ الْعَفُوُّ الرَّءُوفُ مَالِكُ الْمُلْكِ ذُو الْجَـلَالِ وَالإِكْرَام الْمُقْسِطُ الْجَامِعُ الْغَنِيُّ الْمُغْنِي الْمَانِعُ الضَّارُّ النَّافِعُ النُّورُ الْهَادِي الْبَدِيعُ الْبَاقِي الْوَارِثُ الرَّشِيدُ الصَّبُورُ

"Allāh, alladhī lā ilāha illā huwa, ar-Rahmanu, ar-Rahīmu, al-Maliku, al-Quddūsu, as-Salāmu, al-Mu'minu, al-Muhayminu, al-'Azīzu, al-Jabbāru, al-Mutakabbiru, al-Khāliqu, al-Bāri'u, al-Musawwiru, al-Ghaffāru, al-Qahhāru, al-Wahhābu, ar-Razzāqu, al-Fattāhu, al-'Alīmu, al-Qābiḍu, al-Bāsiṭu, al-Khāfiḍu, ar-Rāfi'u, al-Mu'izzu, al-Mudhillu, as-Samī'u, al-Baṣīru, al-Ḥakamu, al-'Adlu, al-Laṭīfu, al-Khabīru, al-Ḥalīmu, al-'Azīmu, al-Ghafūru, ash-Shakūru, al-'Aliyyu, al-Kabīru, al-Ḥafīzu, al-Muqītu, al-Ḥasību, al-Jalīlu, al-Karīmu, ar-Raqību, al-Mujību, al-Wāsi'u, al-Ḥakīmu, al-Wadūdu, al-Majīdu, al-Bā'ithu, ash-Shahīdu, al-Ḥaqqu, al-Wakīlu, al-Qawiyyu, al-Matīnu, al-Waliyyu, al-Ḥamīdu, al-Muḥṣī, al-Mubdi'u, al-Mu'īdu, al-Muhyī, al-Mumītu, al-Ḥayyu, al-Qayyūmu, al-Wājidu, al-Mājidu, al-Wāhidu, aṣ-Ṣamadu, al-Qādiru, al-Muqtadiru, al-Muqaddimu, al-Mu'akhkhiru, al-Awwalu, al-Ākhiru, aẓ-Ẓāhiru, al-Bāṭinu, al-Wālī, al-Muta'ālī, al-Barru, at-Tawwābu, al-Muntaqimu, al-'Afuwwu, ar-Ra'ūfu, Māliku'l-Mulki, Dhu'l-Jalāli Wa'l-Ikrām, al-Muqsiṭu, al-Jāmi'u, al-Ghaniyyu, al-Mughnī, al-Māni'u, aḍ-Ḍārru, an-Nāfi'u, an-Nūru, al-Hādī, al-Badī'u, al-Bāqī, al-Wārithu, ar-Rashīdu, aṣ-Ṣabūru

Allah than whom there is no god, the Compassionate, the Merciful, the King, the Holy, the Source of Peace, the Preserver of security, the Protector, the Mighty, the Overpowering, the Great in Majesty, the Creator, the Maker, the Fashioner, the Forgiver, the Dominant, the Bestower, the

Provider, the Decider, the Knower, the Withholder, the Plentiful Giver, the Abaser, the Exalter, the Honourer, the Humiliator, the Hearer, the Seer, the Judge, the Just, the Gracious, the Aware, the Clement, the Incomparably Great, the All-Forgiving, He Who rewards much, the Exalted, the Great, the Preserver, the Sustainer, the Reckoner, the Majestic, the Generous, the Watcher, the Answerer, the Liberal, the Wise, the Loving, the Glorious, the Raiser, the Witness, the Real, the Trustee, the Strong, the Firm, the Patron, the Praiseworthy, the All-Knowing, the Originator, the Restorer to life, the Giver of life, the Giver of death, the Living, the Eternal, the Self-sufficient, the Grand, the One, He to whom men repair, the Powerful, the Prevailing, the Advancer, the Delayer, the First, the Last, the Outward, the Inward, the Governor, the Sublime, the Amply Beneficent, the Accepter of Penitence, the Avenger, the Pardoner, the Kindly, the Ruler of the Kingdom, the Lord of Majesty and Splendour, the Equitable, the Gatherer, the Independent, the Enricher, the Depriver, the Harmer, the Benefiter, the Light, the Guide, the First Cause, the Enduring, the Inheritor, the Director, the Patient." (Tirmidhī and al-Baihaqī, in *al-Asmā' wa'ṣ-Ṣifāt*)

42

ON SUPPLICATION AND ITS
ACCEPTANCE

Allah, Exalted is He, says: *"When My slaves ask thee concerning Me, I am indeed close (to them): I respond to the prayer of every suppliant when he calleth on Me."* (2: 186)

And He ﷻ says: *"And your Lord says: 'Call on Me; I will answer your (prayer): but those who are too arrogant to serve Me will surely enter Hell abased.'"* (40: 60)

And He ﷻ says: *"Or, who listens to the distressed when he calls on Him, and Who relieves his suffering?"* (27: 62)

476. An-Nu'mān ibn Bashīr ؓ reported that the Prophet ﷺ said, "Supplication is worship itself." (Abū Dāwūd, Tirmidhī)

477. Salmān al-Fārisī ؓ reported Allah's Messenger ﷺ as saying, "Nothing but supplication averts what is decreed, and nothing but beneficence increases life." (Tirmidhī)

478. Abu'd-Dardā' ؓ reported that he heard the Messenger of Allah ﷺ say, "No Muslim slave supplicates for his brother in his absence except that the angel says, 'And for you the same.' " (Muslim)

479. Abū Hurayrah ؓ reported that the Messenger of Allah ﷺ said, "Each of you will be answered as long as he does not get impatient, saying, 'I called on my Lord and He did not answer.' " (Bukhārī, Muslim)

480. Abū Umāmah ⁕ said, "The Messenger of Allah ⁕ was asked, 'What supplication is the most likely to be heard?' He said, 'The supplication made in the middle of the last part of the night and after the obligatory prayers.' " (Tirmidhī)

481. 'Ā'ishah ⁕ said that the Messenger of Allah ⁕ used to prefer comprehensive supplications and abandoned other kinds. (Abū Dāwūd)

482. Anas ibn Mālik ⁕ said that the Prophet's ⁕ most frequent supplication was, اللَّهُمَّ آتِنَا فِي الدُّنْيَا حَسَنَةً وَفِي الآخِرَةِ حَسَنَةً وَقِنَا عَذَابَ النَّارِ *"Allāhumma ātinā fiddunyā ḥasanatan wa fil ākhirati ḥasanatan wa qinā adhābannār – O Allah, bring us blessing in this world, blessing in the next, and guard us from the punishment of the Fire."* (Bukhārī, Muslim)

483. Ibn 'Abbās ⁕ reported that the Messenger of Allah ⁕ used to say in affliction,

لاَ إِلَهَ إِلاَّ اللَّهُ الْعَظِيمُ الْحَلِيمُ لاَ إِلَهَ إِلاَّ اللَّهُ رَبُّ الْعَرْشِ الْعَظِيمِ لاَ إِلَــهَ إِلاَّ اللَّهُ رَبُّ السَّمَوَاتِ وَرَبُّ الأَرْضِ وَرَبُّ الْعَرْشِ الْكَرِيمِ

"Lā ilāha illa'llāhu'l 'aẓīmu'l ḥalīmu lā ilāha illallāhu rabbu'l 'arshi'l 'aẓīmi lā ilāha illallāhu rabbu's-samāwāti wa rabbu'l 'arshi'l 'aẓīm – There is no god but Allah, the Immense, the Forbearing. There is no god but Allah, Lord of the Throne, the Immense. There is no god but Allah, Lord of the heavens, Lord of the earth and Lord of the Throne, the Immense." (Bukhārī, Muslim)

484. Anas ibn Mālik ⁕ said, "The Messenger of Allah ⁕ used to say,

اللَّهُمَّ إِنِّي أَعُوذُ بِكَ مِنَ الْعَجْزِ وَالْكَسَلِ وَالْجُبْنِ وَالْهَرَمِ وَالْبُخْلِ ، وَأَعُوذُ بِكَ مِنْ عَذَابِ الْقَبْرِ، وَأَعُوذُ بِكَ مِنْ فِتْنَةِ الْمَحْيَا وَالْمَمَاتِ

'Allāhumma! Innī a'ūdhu bika mina'l-'ajzi wa'l-kasali wal-jubni wa'l-harami wa'l-bukhli, wa a'ūdhu bika min 'adhābi'l-qabri, wa a'ūdhu bika min fitnati'l-mahyā wa'l-mamāt – O Allah, I seek refuge with You from incapacity, laziness, cowardice, senility and meanness. I seek refuge with You from the punishment of the grave and I seek refuge with You from the trials of life and death.' " (Muslim)

485. Zayd ibn Arqam ﵁ said, "The Messenger of Allah ﷺ used to say,

اللَّهُمَّ إِنِّي أَعُوذُ بِكَ مِنَ الْعَجْزِ وَالْكَسَلِ وَالْجُبْنِ وَالْبُخْلِ وَالْهَرَمِ وَعَــذَابِ الْقَبْرِ ، اللَّهُمَّ آتِ نَفْسِي تَقْوَاهَا وزَكِّهَا ، أَنْتَ خَيْرُ مَنْ زَكَّاهَا ، أَنْـتَ وَلِيُّهَا وَمَوْلاَهَا، اللَّهُمَّ إِنِّي أَعُوذُ بِكَ مِنْ عِلْمٍ لاَ يَنْفَعُ، وَمِــنْ قَلْــبٍ لاَ يَخْشَعُ ، وَمِنْ نَفْسٍ لاَ تَشْبَعُ ، وَمِنْ دَعْوَةٍ لاَ يُسْتَجَابُ لَهَا

'Allāhuma! Innī a'ūdhu bika mina'l-'ajzi wa'l-kasali wa'l-jubni wa'l-bukhli wa'l-harami wa 'adhābi'l qabri. Allāhumma! Āti nafsī taqwāhā wa zakkihā anta khayru man zakkāhā, anta walliyyuhā wa mawlāhā. Allāhumma! Innī a'ūdhu bika min 'ilmin lā yanfa'u wa min qalbin lā yakhsha'u wa min nafsin lā tashba'u wa min da'watin lā yustajābu lahā – O Allah, I seek refuge with You from incapacity, laziness, meanness, senility and the punishment of the grave. O Allah, give my self its taqwā and purify it, You are the best of those who purify it. You are its Master and Guardian. O Allah, I seek refuge with You from knowledge which does not bring benefit and from a heart which is not humble and from a self which is not satisfied and from a supplication which is not answered.' " (Muslim)

486. Ibn 'Abbās ﵄ reported that the Messenger of Allah ﷺ used to say,

اللَّهُمَّ لَكَ أَسْلَمْتُ ، وَبِكَ آمَنْتُ ، وَعَلَيْكَ تَوَكَّلْتُ ، وَإِلَيْكَ أَنَبْتُ ، وَبِكَ خَاصَمْتُ ، وَإِلَيْــكَ حَاكَمْتُ ، فَاغْفِرْ لِي مَا قَدَّمْتُ ، وَمَا أَخَّــرْتُ ، وَمَا أَسْرَرْتُ وَمَا أَعْلَنْتُ ، أَنْتَ الْمُقَدِّمُ وَأَنْــتَ الْمُؤَخِّرُ ، لاَ إِلَهَ إِلاَّ أَنْــتَ ، وَلاَ حَوْلَ وَلاَ قُوَّةَ إِلاَّ بِاللَّه

"Allāhumma! Laka aslamtu wa bika āmantu wa 'alayka tawakkaltu wa ilayka anabtu wa bika khāṣamtu wa ilayka ḥākamtu. Fa'ghfir lī mā qaddamtu wa mā akhkhartu wa mā asrartu wa mā a'lantu. Anta'l-Muqaddimu wa anta'l-mu'akhkhiru. Lā ilāha illā anta, wa lā ḥawla wa lā quwwata illā billāh – O Allah, to You I submit myself and in You I believe. In You I put my trust and to You I turn. By You I argue and take You as arbitrator. Forgive me my past and future wrong actions and what I keep secret and what I make known. You are the One who puts forward and defers. There is no god but You, and there is no power (to avert evil) or strength (to do good) but by Allah." (Bukhārī, Muslim)

487. Abū Hurayrah ؓ reported that the Messenger of Allah ﷺ used to say,

اللَّهُمَّ أَصْلِحْ لِي دِينِي الَّذِي هُوَ عِصْمَةُ أَمْرِي ، وَأَصْلِحْ لِي دُنْيَايَ الَّتِي فِيهَا مَعَاشِي ، وَأَصْلِحْ لِي آخِرَتِي الَّتِي فِيهَا مَعَادِي ، وَاجْعَلْ الْحَيَاةَ زِيَادَةً لِي فِي كُلِّ خَيْرٍ ، وَاجْعَلْ الْمَوْتَ رَاحَةً لِي مِنْ كُلِّ شَرٍّ

"Allāhumma! Aṣliḥ lī dīnī alladhī huwa 'iṣmatu amrī wa aṣliḥ lī dunyāya allatī fīhā ma'āshī wa aṣliḥ lī ākhirati allatī fīhā ma'ādī wa'j'ali'l-ḥayāta ziyādatan lī fī kulli khayrin wa'j'ali'l-mawta rāḥatan lī min kulli sharr – O Allah, put right for me my dīn in which lies the protection of my affair and put right for me this world in which lies my livelihood and put right for me the Next World to which is my return. Make life for me an increase in every good and make death for me a rest from every evil." (Muslim)

488. Abū Umāmah ؓ said, "The Messenger of Allah ﷺ made many supplications which we did not remember at all. We said, 'Messenger of Allah, you have made many supplications which we do not remember at all.' He said, 'Shall I tell you something which will contain all of them for you? You should say,

اللَّهُمَّ إِنِّي أَسْأَلُكَ مِنْ خَيْرِ مَا سَأَلَكَ مِنْهُ نَبِيُّكَ مُحَمَّدٌ – صَلَّى اللَّهُ عَلَيْهِ وَسَلَّمَ – وَنَعُوذُ بِكَ مِنْ شَرِّ مَا اسْتَعَاذَ مِنْهُ نَبِيُّكَ مُحَمَّدٌ – صَلَّى اللَّهُ عَلَيْهِ وَسَلَّمَ – وَأَنْتَ الْمُسْتَعَانُ ، وَعَلَيْكَ الْبَلَاغُ ، وَلَا حَوْلَ وَلَا قُوَّةَ إِلَّا بِاللَّهِ

"Allāhumma! Innī as'aluka min khayri mā sa'alaka minhu nabiyyuka Muḥammadun ﷺ, wa a'ūdhu bika min sharri ma'sta'ādhaka minhu nabiyyuka Muḥammadun ﷺ, wa anta'l-musta'ānu wa 'alayka'l-balāghu wa la ḥawla wa lā quwwata illā billāh – O Allah, I ask You for the good for which Your Prophet Muḥammad ﷺ asked You and I seek refuge from the evil from which Your Prophet Muḥammad ﷺ sought refuge. You are the One who is asked for help and it is only You who can transmit it. There is no power nor strength except by Allah." ' " (Tirmidhī)

489. 'Abdullāh ibn Buraidah ؓ narrated from his father that Allah's Messenger ﷺ heard a man saying,

اللَّهُمَّ إِنِّي أَسْأَلُكَ بِأَنِّي أَشْهَدُ أَنَّكَ أَنْتَ اللَّهُ لَا إِلَهَ إِلَّا أَنْتَ الْأَحَدُ الصَّمَدُ الَّذِي لَمْ يَلِدْ وَلَمْ يُولَدْ وَلَمْ يَكُنْ لَهُ كُفُوًا أَحَدٌ

"Allāhuma! Innī ashhadu annaka anta'l-lāhu lā ilāha illā anta, al-Aḥadu aṣ'-Ṣamadu, alladhī lam yalid wa lam yūlad, wa lam yakun lahū kufuwan aḥad - O Allah, I bear witness that You are Allah other than whom there is no god, the One, the Eternal, who did not give birth, nor was He born, and there is none like unto Him." Allah's Messenger then said, "You have asked Allah by the name which when asked by it He gives, and when supplicated by it He answers." (Abū Dāwūd, Tirmidhī)

490. Sa'd ibn Abī Waqqāṣ ﷺ reported that Allah's Messenger ﷺ said, "The supplication of Dhu'n-Nūn (Yūnus, pbuh) while he was inside the belly of the whale was, لاَ إِلَهَ إِلاَّ أَنْتَ سُبْحَانَكَ إِنِّي كُنْتُ مِنَ الظَّالِمِينَ *'Lā ilāha illā anta subḥānaka innī kuntu min'aẓ-ẓālimīn – There is no god but You, Glory be to You, surely I was one of the wrongdoers.'* (21: 87) Whenever a Muslim man asks Allah for something with this supplication, Allah will certainly answer him." (an-Nasā'ī, Tirmidhī)

491. Jābir ibn 'Abdullāh ﷺ said, "The Messenger of Allah ﷺ said, 'Do not curse each other, do not curse your children, do not curse your servants, and do not curse your property lest it should coincide with a time from Allah in which gifts that are asked for are granted." (Muslim, Abū Dāwūd)

43

COMPENDIUM OF INVOCATIONS
AND SPECIAL SUPPLICATIONS

492. Hudhayfah and Abū Dharr 🌸 said: "When the Messenger of Allah 🌸 intended to sleep, he would say, بِاسْمِكَ اللَّهُمَّ أَمُوتُ وَا *Bismika, Allāhumma! Amūtu wa aḥyā – In Your name, O Allah, I die and live.'* When he awoke he would say, الْحَمْدُ لِلّٰهِ الَّذِي أَحْيَانَا بَعْدَ مَا أَمَاتَنَا وَإِلَيْهِ النُّشُورُ *'Al-ḥamdu lillāhi'l-ladhī aḥyānā ba'da mā amātanā wa ilayhi'n-nushūr – Praise be to Allah who has given us life after causing us to die, and to Whom is the resurrection.'* " (Bukhārī, Muslim)

493. Ibn 'Abbās 🌸 narrated that Allah's Messenger 🌸 said, "If any of you who means to have intercourse with his wife says, بِاسْمِ اللَّهِ اللَّهُمَّ جَنِّبْنَا الشَّيْطَانَ وَجَنِّبْ الشَّيْطَانَ مَا رَزَقْتَنَا *'Bismillāhi. Allāhumma! Jannibna'sh-shayṭāna, wa jannibi'sh-shayṭāna mā razaqtanā – In the name of Allah. O Allah, keep us away from the Shayṭān and keep the Shayṭān away from what You provide us'*, should it be decreed that a child be born to them thereby, he will never harm it." (Bukhārī, Muslim)

494. Abū Hurayrah 🌸 reported that the Prophet 🌸 used to say in the morning, اللَّهُمَّ بِكَ أَصْبَحْنَا وَبِكَ أَمْسَيْنَا ، وَبِكَ نَحْيَا وَبِكَ نَمُوتُ ، وَإِلَيْكَ النُّشُورُ *"Allāhumma! Bika aṣbaḥnā wa bika amsaynā wa bika naḥyā wa bika namūtu wa ilayka'n-Nushūr – O Allah, by You we start the day and by You we end it, by You we live and by You we die, and to You is the gathering."* (Abū Dāwūd, Tirmidhī)

495. Anas ibn Mālik 🌸 narrated, "Whenever the Prophet 🌸 went to the lavatory, he used to say, اللَّهُمَّ إِنِّي أَعُوذُ بِكَ مِنَ الْخُبُثِ وَالْخَبَائِثِ *'Allāhumma! Innī a'ūdhu bika mina'l-khubuthi wa'l-khabā'ith – O Allah, I seek refuge with You from male and female demons.'* " (Bukhārī)

496. Abū Umāmah ❧ said that when the cloth, upon which his meal was laid, was removed (upon finishing eating) the Prophet ﷺ used to say, الْحَمْدُ للهِ كَثِيرًا طَيِّبًا مُبَارَكًا فِيهِ غَيْرَ مَكْفِيٍّ وَلاَ مُوَدَّعٍ وَلاَ مُسْتَغْنًى عَنْهُ رَبَّنَا "*Al-ḥamdu li'llāhi kathīran ṭayyiban mubārakan fīhi, ghayra makfiyyin wa lā muwadda'in wa lā mustaghnan 'anhu, rabbanā! – Praise be to Allah abundantly, and wholesomely, of such a nature as is productive of blessing. Your favour can not be compensated, nor can be left, nor can be dispensed with, O our Lord!*" (Bukhārī)

497. Abū Sa'īd al-Khudrī ❧ said, "When the Messenger of Allah ﷺ put on a new garment, whether it was a turban, shirt or cloak, he would name it and say,

اللَّهُمَّ لَكَ الْحَمْدُ أَنْتَ كَسَوْتَنِيهِ أَسْأَلُكَ خَيْرَهُ وَخَيْرَ مَا صُنِعَ لَهُ وَأَعُوذُ بِكَ مِنْ شَرِّهِ وَشَرِّ مَا صُنِعَ لَهُ

'*Allāhumma! Laka'l-ḥamdu, anta kasawtanīhi, as'aluka khayrahū wa khayra mā ṣuni'a lahū, wa a'ūdhu bika min sharrīhī wa sharri mā ṣuni'a lahū – O Allah, praise be to You. You have clothed me with it. I ask you for the good of it and the good of what it was made for. I seek refuge with You from its evil and the evil of what it was made for.*' " (Abū Dāwūd, Tirmidhī)

498. Umm Salamah ❧ said that when the Prophet ﷺ went out of his house he said,

بِسْمِ اللهِ تَوَكَّلْتُ عَلَى اللهِ اللَّهُمَّ إِنَّا نَعُوذُ بِكَ مِنْ أَنْ نَزِلَّ أَوْ نَضِلَّ أَوْ نَظْلِمَ أَوْ نُظْلَمَ أَوْ نَجْهَلَ أَوْ يُجْهَلَ عَلَيْنَا

"*Bismi'llāhi tawakkaltu 'ala'llāh. Allāhumma! Innā na'ūdhu bika min an nazilla aw naḍilla aw naẓlima aw nuẓlama aw najhala aw yujhala 'alynā – In the name of Allah; I trust in Allah; O Allah, we seek refuge in You from slipping, or straying, or causing injustice, or suffering injustice, or acting foolishly, or that others act foolishly to us.*" (Tirmidhī)

499. Ibn 'Umar ❧ reported that when the Messenger of Allah ﷺ was sitting on his camel ready to go on a journey, he would say, "*Allāhu Akbar – Allah is most great*" three times. Then he said,

سُبْحَانَ الَّذِي سَخَّرَ لَنَا هَذَا وَمَا كُنَّا لَهُ مُقْرِنِينَ وَإِنَّا إِلَى رَبِّنَا لَمُنْقَلِبُونَ اللَّهُمَّ إِنَّا نَسْأَلُكَ فِي سَفَرِنَا هَذَا الْبِرَّ وَالتَّقْوَى وَمِنْ الْعَمَلِ مَا تَرْضَى اللَّهُمَّ هَوِّنْ عَلَيْنَا سَفَرَنَا هَذَا وَاطْوِ عَنَّا بُعْدَهُ اللَّهُمَّ أَنْتَ

الصَّاحِبُ فِي السَّفَرِ وَالْخَلِيفَةُ فِي الأَهْلِ اللَّهُمَّ إِنِّي أَعُوذُ بِكَ مِنْ وَعْثَاءِ السَّفَرِ وَكَآبَةِ الْمَنْظَرِ وَسُوءِ الْمُنْقَلَبِ فِي الْمَالِ وَالأَهْلِ

"Subḥāna'l-ladhī sakhkara lanā hādhā wa mā kunnā lahū muqrinīna, wa innā ilā rabbinā lamunqalibūn. Allāhumma! Innā nas'aluka fī safarina hādhā al-birra wa'ttaqwā wa mina'l-'amali mā tarḍā – Glorified be He who subjected this to us, and we were not capable [of subjecting it], and to our Lord we are returning." (43: 13–14)

"Allāhumma! Hawwin 'alaynā safaranā hādhā wa'ṭwi 'annā bu'dahu. Allāhumma! Anta'ṣ-ṣāḥibu fi's-safari wa'l-khalīfatu fi'l-ahli. Allāhumma! Innī a'ūdhu bika min wa'thā'is-safari wa ka'ābati'l-manẓari wa sū'i'l-munqalabi fi'l-māli wa'l-ahli – O Allah, we ask You in this journey of ours for uprightness, taqwā and such deeds as are pleasing to You. O Allah, make this journey of ours easy for us and make its length short for us. O Allah, You are the Companion in the Journey and the Successor (and Guardian) of the family. O Allah, I seek refuge with You from the difficulty of travelling, the bad and undesirable things that I may see, and from finding that harm has come when I return to my property and family." Upon returning from a journey he would say the same words, adding: آيِبُونَ تَائِبُونَ عَابِدُونَ لِرَبِّنَا حَامِدُونَ *"Ā'ibūna, tā'ibūna, 'ābidūna li rabbinā ḥāmidūna – [We are] Returning, repentant, worshipping, [and] to our Lord praising."* (Muslim)

500. Abū Hurayrah ﵁ told of a man who said, "Messenger of Allah ﷺ, I intend to make a journey, so advise me." He told him, "Have fear of Allah and say, *Allahu Akbar – Allah is most great* on every rising ground", and when the man turned away he said, اللَّهُمَّ اطْوِ لَهُ الأَرْضَ وَهَوِّنْ عَلَيْهِ السَّفَرَ *"Allāhumma! Iṭwi lahu'l-arḍa wa hawwin 'alayhi's-safara – O Allah, make the distance short for him and make the journey easy for him."* (Tirmidhī)

501. Ibn 'Umar ﵄ used to say to a man when he meant to travel, "Come close to me so that I can bid you farewell as the Messenger of Allah ﷺ used to bid us farewell." Then he would say, أَسْتَوْدِعُ اللَّهَ دِينَكَ وَأَمَانَتَكَ وَخَوَاتِيمَ عَمَلِكَ *"Astawdi'u'l-lāha dīnaka wa amānataka wa khawātīma a'mālika – I entrust to Allah your dīn, what you are responsible for and your life's concluding deeds."* (Tirmidhī)

502. Abū Hurayrah ﷺ said, "The Messenger of Allah ﷺ said, 'Whoever sees someone who is suffering affliction and says, الْحَمْدُ لِلّٰه الَّذي عَافَاني ممَّا ابْتَلاكَ به وَفَضَّلَني عَلَى كَثير ممَّنْ خَلَقَ تَفْضيلا "*Al-ḥamdu li'llāhi'l-ladhī 'āfānī min ma'btalāka bihī, wa faḍḍalanī 'alā kathīrin mimman khalaqa tafḍīlā – Praise be to Allah who has kept me free from that which He has tested you with, and has shown me favour above many whom He has created*", that affliction will not smite him.' " (Tirmidhī)

503. 'Ā'ishah ﷺ said, "When the weather was stormy the Prophet ﷺ would say,

اللّهُمَّ إنّي أَسْأَلُكَ مِنْ خَيْرِهَا وَخَيْرِ مَا فِيهَا وَخَيْرِ مَا أُرْسِلَتْ بِهِ وَأَعُوذُ بِكَ مِنْ شَرِّهَا وَشَرِّ مَا فِيهَا وَشَرِّ مَا أُرْسِلَتْ بِهِ

'Allāhumma! Innī as'aluka min khayrihā wa khayri mā fīhā wa khayri mā ursilat bihī wa a'ūdhu bika min sharrihā wa sharri mā fīhā wa sharri mā ursilat bihī – O Allah, I ask You for its good, the good of what is in it and the good of what it was sent for, and I seek refuge in You from its mischief, the mischief of what is in it and the mischief of what it was sent for.' " (Tirmidhī)

504. 'Ā'ishah ﷺ said, "When the Messenger of Allah ﷺ saw it raining he would say, اللّهُمَّ صَيِّبًا نَافعًا *'Allāhumma! Ṣayban nāfi'an – O Allah [make it] a beneficial downpour.'* " (Bukhārī, Muslim)

505. Talḥah ibn 'Ubaydullāh ﷺ narrated that when the Prophet ﷺ saw the new moon he used to say, اللّهُمَّ أَهْلِلْهُ عَلَيْنَا بِالْيُمْنِ وَالإيمَانِ وَالسَّلامَةِ وَالإسْلامِ رَبِّي وَرَبُّكَ اللّٰهُ *"Allāhumma! Ahillahū 'alaynā bi'l yumni wal-īmāni wa's-salāmati wa'l-islāmi. Rabbī wa rabbuka'l-lāh – O Allah, make the new moon rise on us, with security, faith, safety and Islam. My Lord and your Lord is Allah."* (Tirmidhī)

506. 'Ā'ishah ﷺ said that the Prophet ﷺ was visiting a family member who was ill. He wiped him with his right hand and prayed: اللّهُمَّ أَذْهِبْ الْبَأْسَ رَبَّ النَّاسِ وَاشْفِ فَأَنْتَ الشَّافي لا شفَاءَ إلاَّ شفَاؤُكَ شفَاءً لا يُغَادرُ سَقَمًا *"Allāhumma! Rabba'n-nāsi! Adhhibi'l ba'sa wa'shfi anta'sh shāfī lā shifā'a illā shifā'uka, shifā'an lā yughādiru saqamā – O Allah, Lord of mankind, remove the harm, and heal, You are the Healer. There is no healing but Yours, a healing which leaves no illness behind."* (Bukhārī, Muslim)

507. It is reported that Anas ﷺ said to Thābit, "Shall I not charm you with the charm of the Messenger of Allah (ﷺ)?" He said, "Yes." Anas said, it is, اللَّهُمَّ رَبَّ النَّاسِ مُذْهِبَ الْبَاسِ اشْفِ أَنْتَ الشَّافِي لاَ شَافِيَ إِلاَّ أَنْتَ شِفَاءً لاَ يُغَادِرُ سَقَمًا *"Allāhumma! Rabba'n-nāsi, Mudhhiba'l bā'si! Ishfi ana'sh-shāfī lā shāfiya illā anta shifā'an la yughādiru saqamā – O Allah, Lord of people, remover of hardship, heal – for You are the Healer other than whom there is no healer – with a healing that does not leave illness behind."* (Bukhārī)

508. Abū Sa'īd al-Khudrī ﷺ reported that Jibrīl, peace be upon him, came to the Prophet (ﷺ) and said, "Muḥammad, are you in pain?" He said, "Yes." He said, بِاسْمِ اللّٰهِ أَرْقِيكَ مِنْ كُلِّ شَيْءٍ يُؤْذِيكَ مِنْ شَرِّ كُلِّ نَفْسٍ أَوْ عَيْنِ حَاسِدٍ اللّٰهُ يَشْفِيكَ بِاسْمِ اللّٰهِ أَرْقِيكَ *"Bismi'llāhi arqīka, min kulli shay'in yu'dhīka, min sharri kulli nafsin aw 'aynin ḥāsidin, Allāhu yashfīka – In the name of Allah, I charm you against everything that might harm you, the evil of every envious self or eye. May Allah heal you. In the name of Allah, I charm you."* (Muslim)

509. Abū Hurayrah ﷺ said, "A man came to Allah's Messenger (ﷺ) and said, 'Messenger of Allah, how badly I have suffered from a scorpion which stung me last night!' He replied, 'If you had said in the evening, أَعُوذُ بِكَلِمَاتِ اللّٰهِ التَّامَّاتِ مِنْ شَرِّ مَا خَلَقَ *"A'ūdhu bi kalimāti'l-lāhi't-tāmmāti min sharri mā khalaqa – I seek refuge in Allah's perfect words from the evil of what He has created,"* it would not have harmed you.' " (Muslim)

510. 'Abdullāh ibn Khubayb ﷺ said, "Allah's Messenger (ﷺ) said to me, 'Read sūrahs *Qul Huwa'llāhu Aḥad* and *al-Mu'awwidhatain* (*Qul a'ūdhū bi rabbi'l falaq* and *Qul a'ūdhū bi rabbi'n nās*) three times morning and evening, they will suffice you for every purpose (protect you from every mischief).' " (Abū Dāwūd, Tirmidhī)

511. 'Uthmān ibn 'Affān ﷺ said, "Allah's Messenger (ﷺ) said to me, 'If any slave [of Allah] says upon the morning of every day and on the evening of every night: بِسْمِ اللّٰهِ الَّذِي لاَ يَضُرُّ مَعَ اسْمِهِ شَيْءٌ فِي الأَرْضِ وَلاَ فِي السَّمَاءِ وَهُوَ السَّمِيعُ الْعَلِيمُ *"Bismi'llāhi'l-ladhī lā yaḍurru ma'a'smihī shay'un fi'l-arḍi wa lā fi's-samā'i, wa huwa's-samī'ul-'alīm – In the name of Allah, the One along with Whose name nothing in earth or heaven can cause harm, and He is the Hearer, the Knower,"* three times, he will not be harmed by anything.' " (Abū Dāwūd, Tirmidhī)

512. 'Alī ibn Abī Ṭālib ﷺ said that a slave, who had made a contract with his master to pay for his freedom, came to him and said, "I am unable to fulfil my contract, so help me." He said, "Shall I not teach you some words which Allah's Messenger ﷺ taught me, and which even if you had a debt as large as a mountain Allah would pay it for you?: اللَّهُمَّ اكْفِنِي بِحَلاَلِكَ عَنْ حَرَامِكَ وَأَغْنِنِي بِفَضْلِكَ عَمَّنْ سِوَاكَ *'Allāhumma! Ikfinī bi ḥalālika 'an ḥarāmika wa aghninī bi faḍlika 'an man siwāka – O Allah, grant me enough of what You make lawful that I may dispense with what You make unlawful, and make me independent, by Your bounty, of other than You.'* " (Tirmidhī)

513. Abū Sa'īd al-Khudrī ﷺ reported that Allah's Messenger ﷺ said to Abū Umāmah, "Shall I not teach you words which, when you say them, Allah will remove your care and settle your debt?" Abū Umāmah said, "Certainly! Messenger of Allah." He said, "Say morning and evening,

اللَّهُمَّ إِنِّي أَعُوذُ بِكَ مِنْ الْهَمِّ وَالْحَزَنِ وَأَعُوذُ بِكَ مِنْ الْعَجْزِ وَالْكَسَلِ وَأَعُوذُ بِكَ مِنْ الْجُبْنِ وَالْبُخْلِ وَأَعُوذُ بِكَ مِنْ غَلَبَةِ الدَّيْنِ وَقَهْرِ الرِّجَالِ

'Allāhumma! Innī a'ūdhu bika mina'l-hammi wa'l-ḥazan wa a'ūdhu bika mina'l 'ajzi wa'l-kasali wa a'ūdhu bika mina'l bukhli wa'l-jubni wa a'ūdhu bika min ghalabati'd-dayni wa qahri'r-rijāli – O Allah, I seek refuge with You from care and grief; I seek refuge with You from incapacity and laziness; I seek refuge with You from meanness and cowardice; I seek refuge with You from being overcome by debt and overpowered by men.' " He said, "I said that, and Allah removed my care and settled my debt." (Abū Dāwūd)

514. Ibn 'Abbās ﷺ said, "The Messenger of Allah ﷺ said, 'If someone clings to asking for forgiveness, Allah will appoint him a way out of every constriction, and relief from every care and will provide for him from where he does not reckon.' " (Abū Dāwūd, an-Nasā'ī and Ibn Mājah)

515. 'Ā'ishah ﷺ said that when a person complained of some trouble, or if he had a sore or a wound, the Prophet ﷺ would say, putting his finger just so, [while narrating this *ḥadīth*] Sufyān (ibn 'Uyaynah) put his index finger on the earth then raised it:

بِاسْمِ اللَّهِ تُرْبَةُ أَرْضِنَا بِرِيقَةِ بَعْضِنَا لِيُشْفَى بِهِ سَقِيمُنَا بِإِذْنِ رَبِّنَا *"Bismillāhi turbatu arḍinā bi rīqati ba'ḍinā li yushfā bihī saqīmunā, bi idhni rabbinā – In the name of Allah. It is the soil of our land with the spittle of one of us, that our sick one may be healed by it by our Lord's permission."* (Muslim)

516. 'Uthmān ibn Abi'l 'Āṣ ath-Thaqafī ﷺ said that he complained to Allah's Messenger ﷺ of a pain he had in his body ever since he had become a Muslim. The Messenger of Allah ﷺ said to him, "Put your hand on the part of your body which is sore and say three times: *Bis'millāh – In the name of Allah*, and seven times, أَعُوذُ بِاللَّهِ وَقُدْرَتِهِ مِنْ شَرِّ مَا أَجِدُ وَأُحَاذِرُ *'A'ūdhu bi'llāhi wa qudratihī min sharri mā ajidu wa uḥādhiru – I seek refuge in Allah and in His power from the mischief of what I am experiencing and trying to avert.'* " (Muslim)

517. 'Uthmān b. Ḥunayf ﷺ related how a blind man came to the Messenger of Allah ﷺ and said, "Messenger of Allah, ask Allah to remove the veil from my sight." He replied, "If you wish, I shall make supplication to Allah, but if you wish you will endure, for that is better for you." The man said, "Messenger of Allah, it has been a great hardship to me to lose my sight." He said, "Go and perform *wuḍū'*, doing it well, then pray two *rak'ahs* and say,

اللَّهُمَّ إِنِّي أَسْأَلُكَ وَأَتَوَجَّهُ إِلَيْكَ بِنَبِيِّكَ مُحَمَّدٍ نَبِيِّ الرَّحْمَةِ يَا مُحَمَّدُ إِنِّي أَتَوَجَّهُ إِلَى رَبِّي بِكَ أَنْ يَكْشِفَ لِي بَصَرِي اللَّهُمَّ فَشَفِّعْهُ فِيَّ وَشَفِّعْنِي فِي نَفْسِي

'Allāhumma! Innī as'aluka wa atawajjahu ilayka bi nabiyyika Muḥammadin nabiyyi'r-raḥmati. Yā Muḥammadu! Innī atawajjahu ilā rabbī bika an yakshifa lī baṣarī. Allāhumma! Shaffi'hu fiyya wa shaffi'nī fī nafsī – O Allah, I ask You and I turn towards You by means of Your Prophet Muḥammad, the Prophet of mercy. O Muḥammad, by means of you I have turned towards my Lord to accomplish for me this need of mine. O Allah, make him an intercessor for me and make me an intercessor for myself', and he returned and his sight had come back." (Tirmidhī, an-Nasā'ī and Kitāb ash-Shifā')

518. Jābir ibn 'Abdullāh ﷺ said, "Allah's Messenger ﷺ used to teach us how to ask for Allah's guidance [in a matter] just as he used to teach us a *sūrah* of the Qur'ān, saying, 'When any of you is

concerned about something (he intends to do), he should pray two *rak'ahs* (apart from the obligatory prayers). Then let him say:

اللَّهُمَّ إِنِّي أَسْتَخِيرُكَ بِعِلْمِكَ وَأَسْتَقْدِرُكَ بِقُدْرَتِكَ وَأَسْأَلُكَ مِنْ فَضْلِكَ الْعَظِيمِ فَإِنَّكَ تَقْدِرُ وَلاَ أَقْدِرُ وَتَعْلَمُ وَلاَ أَعْلَمُ وَأَنْتَ عَلاَّمُ الْغُيُوبِ اللَّهُمَّ إِنْ كُنْتَ تَعْلَمُ أَنَّ **هَذَا الأَمْرَ** خَيْرٌ لِي فِي دِينِي وَمَعَاشِي وَعَاقِبَةِ أَمْرِي – فِي عَاجِلِ أَمْرِي وَآجِلِهِ – فَاقْدُرْهُ لِي وَإِنْ كُنْتَ تَعْلَمُ أَنَّ **هَذَا الأَمْرَ** شَرٌّ لِي فِي دِينِي وَمَعَاشِي وَعَاقِبَةِ أَمْرِي – فِي عَاجِلِ أَمْرِي وَآجِلِهِ – فَاصْرِفْهُ عَنِّي وَاصْرِفْنِي عَنْهُ وَاقْدُرْ لِي الْخَيْرَ حَيْثُ كَانَ ثُمَّ رَضِّنِي بِهِ

Allāhumma! Innī astakhīruka bi 'ilmika wa 'astqdiruka bi qudratika wa as-aluka min faḍlika'l-'aẓīm. Fa innaka taqdiru wa lā aqdiru wa ta'lamu wa lā a'lamu wa anta 'allāmu'l-ghuyūb. Allāhumma! In kunta ta'lamu anna ***hādha'l-amra*** *khayrun lī fī dīnī wa ma'āshī wa 'āqibati amrī – fī 'ājili amrī wa 'ājilihī – fa'qdurhu lī, wa in kunta ta'lamu anna* ***hādha'l-amra*** *sharrun lī fī dīnī wa ma'āshī wa 'āqibati amrī – fī 'ājili amrī wa 'ājilihī – fa'ṣrifhu 'annī wa'srifnī 'anhu wa'qdur liya'l-kayra ḥaythu kāna thumma raḍḍinī bihī – O Allah, I ask You [to guide my] choice by Your knowledge, I ask You for strength by Your power, and I ask You of Your great favour, for You have power and I have none, You know and I do not, and You are the One Who is fully Knowing of unseen matters. O Allah, if You know that* **this matter** (and one should name the matter) *is good for me regarding my dīn, my livelihood, and the outcome of my affair, (or "in its immediate consequences and its final term"), decree it for me and make it easy for me, then bless me in it. But if You know that* ***this matter*** *is bad for me regarding my religion, my livelihood, and the outcome of my affair (or "in its immediate consequences and its final term"), turn it away from me, turn me away from it, and decree the good for me wherever it is, then make me pleased with it.'"* (Bukhārī)

44

ON REPENTANCE AND ASKING FOR FORGIVENESS

Allah, Exalted is He, says: *"O ye who believe! Turn to Allah with sincere repentance."* (66: 8)

And He ﷻ says: *"And O ye believers! Turn ye all together towards Allah in repentance that ye may be successful."* (24: 31)

And He ﷻ says: *"If any one does evil or wrongs his own soul but afterwards seeks Allah's forgiveness, he will find Allah Oft-forgiving, Most Merciful."* (4: 110)

And He ﷻ says: *"And those who, having done an act of indecency or wronged their own souls, remember Allah and ask for forgiveness for their sins – and who can forgive sins except Allah?"* (3: 135)

And He ﷻ says: *"But Allah was not going to send a Chastisement whilst thou wast amongst them; nor was He going to send it whilst they could ask for pardon."* (8: 33)

519. Abū Hurayrah ؓ said, "I heard the Messenger of Allah ﷺ say, 'By Allah, I ask Allah's forgiveness and repent to Him more than seventy times a day." (Bukhārī)

520. Al-Agharr al-Muzanī ؓ reported that the Messenger of Allah ﷺ said, "A Gloominess comes over my heart and I ask for Allah's forgiveness a hundred times a day." (Muslim)

521. Ibn 'Umar ؓ said, "We used to count the Messenger of Allah ﷺ saying in one assembly a hundred times (the following

supplication), رَبِّ اغْفِرْ لِي وَتُبْ عَلَيَّ إِنَّكَ أَنْتَ التَّوَّابُ الرَّحِيمُ *Rabbi'ghfir lī wa tub 'alayya innaka anta't-tawwābu'r-raḥīm – Lord forgive me and turn to me, truly You are the most forgiving, the Merciful.*" (Abū Dāwūd)

522. Abū Mūsā 'Abdullāh ibn Qays al-Ash'arī ﷺ reported that the Prophet ﷺ said, "Allah, Exalted is He, stretches out His hand during the night, so that the one who did wrong during the day can turn (to Him), and stretches out His hand during the day, so that the one who did wrong during the night can turn (to Him), until (the day) the sun rises from the place it set." (Muslim)

523. 'Abdullāh ibn 'Umar ibn al-Khaṭṭāb ﷺ reported that the Prophet ﷺ said, "Allah the Mighty and Majestic accepts the repentance of the slave as long as his death-rattle has not begun." (Tirmidhī)

524. Anas ibn Mālik ﷺ said, "Allah's Messenger ﷺ said, 'All the children of Adam make mistakes but the best of those who make mistakes are those who often repent.' " (Tirmidhī, Ibn Mājah and Dārimī)

525. Abū Hurayrah ﷺ reported Allah's Messenger ﷺ as saying, "When the slave does wrong, a black spot is stamped in his heart and if he regrets it, asks pardon and repents, his heart becomes polished; but if he returns (to his wrong) the black spots increase till his heart is covered. That is the rust mentioned by Allah, *'Nay, but what they were committing has spread like rust over their hearts.'* " (83: 14) (Tirmidhī, Aḥmad and Ibn Mājah)

526. Ibn 'Abbās ﷺ said, "The Messenger of Allah ﷺ said, 'If someone clings to asking for forgiveness, Allah will make for him a way out of any constriction, and relief from any care and will provide for him from where he does not expect.' " (Abū Dāwūd)

527. Bilāl ibn Yasār ibn Zayd reported on his father's authority that, "Allah's Messenger ﷺ said, 'If anyone says, أَسْتَغْفِرُ اللَّهَ الَّذِي لَا إِلَهَ إِلَّا هُوَ الْحَيَّ الْقَيُّومُ وَأَتُوبُ إِلَيْهِ *"Astaghfiru'l-lāha'l-ladhī lā ilāha*

illā huwa'l ḥayyu'l-qayyūmu wa atūbu ilayh – I ask forgiveness of Allah beside whom there is no god, the Living, the Subsistent, and I turn to Him in repentance," he will be pardoned, even if he has fled in time of battle.' " (Tirmidhī, Abū Dāwūd)

528. Shaddād ibn Aws ☙ said, "Allah's Messenger ﷺ said, 'The best way of asking for forgiveness is that the slave says:

اللَّهُمَّ أَنْتَ رَبِّي لَا إِلَهَ إِلاَّ أَنْتَ خَلَقْتَنِي وَأَنَا عَبْدُكَ وَأَنَا عَلَى عَهْدِكَ وَوَعْدِكَ مَا اسْتَطَعْتُ أَعُوذُ بِكَ مِنْ شَرِّ مَا صَنَعْتُ أَبُوءُ لَكَ بِنِعْمَتِكَ عَلَيَّ وَأَبُوءُ لَكَ بِذَنْبِي فَاغْفِرْ لِي فَإِنَّهُ لاَ يَغْفِرُ الذُّنُوبَ إِلاَّ أَنْتَ

"Allāhumma! Anta Rabbī, Lā ilāha illā anta, khalaqani wa anā 'abduka wa anā 'alā 'ahdika wa wa'dika ma'stata'tu. A 'ūdhu bika min sharri mā ṣana'tu. Abū'u laka bi ni'ma-tika 'alayya, wa abū'u laka bi dhambī; fa'gfir lī, fa innahū lā ya'gfiru'dh-dhunūba illā anta – O Allah, You are my Lord. There is no god but You. You created me, and I am Your slave and hold to Your covenant and promise as much as I can. I seek refuge in You from the mischief of what I have done. I acknowledge Your favour to me, and I acknowledge my wrong action, so pardon me, for none pardons wrong actions but You." Whoever says it during the day, certain of it, and dies before night is one of the people of the Garden and whoever says it during the night, certain of it, and dies that night before morning is one of the people of the Garden.' " (Bukhārī)

45

ON ṢALĀT ‘ALA’N-NABĪ ﷺ

Allah, Exalted is He, says: *"Allah and His Angels, send blessings on the Prophet: O ye that believe! Send ye blessings on him, and salute him with all respect."* (33: 56)

529. ‘Amr ibn al-‘Āṣ ؓ said, "I heard the Messenger of Allah ﷺ say, ‘Anyone who invokes blessings on me, Allah will bless him ten times on account of it.’ " (Muslim)

530. ‘Abdullāh ibn Mas‘ūd ؓ reported that the Messenger of Allah ﷺ said, "The closest of people to me on the Day of Rising will be the ones who invoke blessing on me the most." (Tirmidhī)

531. Abū Hurayrah ؓ reported that the Messenger of Allah ﷺ said, "May humiliation be the lot of any man who, when I am mentioned in his presence, does not invoke blessing on me." (Tirmidhī)

532. Abū Hurayrah ؓ reported that the Messenger of Allah ﷺ said, "Do not make my grave a place of celebration, and invoke blessing on me, because your invocation of blessings reaches me wherever you are." (Abū Dāwūd)

533. Aws ibn Aws ؓ said, "The Messenger of Allah ﷺ said, ‘One of the best of your days is the Day of *Jumu‘ah*, so invoke a lot of blessings on me during it. For your invocation of blessing is shown to me." They said, "Messenger of Allah, how will our invocation of blessings be shown to you when you have become

dust?". He said, "Allah has forbidden the earth (to consume) the bodies of the Prophets." (Abū Dāwūd)

534. 'Abdullāh ibn 'Amr ibn al-'Āṣ ﵁ reported that he heard Allah's Messenger ﷺ saying, "When you hear the *mu'adhdhin* repeat what he says, then invoke blessing on me, for, everyone who invokes a blessing on me, Allah will send ten blessings on him for it. Then ask Allah to give me the *wasīlah*, which is a degree in the Garden which will only be granted to one of Allah's slaves, and I hope that I may be him. If anyone asks that I be given the *wasīlah* he will be assured of [my] intercession." (Muslim, Abū Dāwūd and Tirmidhī)

535. Ubayy ibn Ka'b ﵁ said, "I said, 'Allah's Messenger, ﷺ I frequently invoke blessings on you. How much of my prayer should I devote to you?' He replied, 'As much as you wish.' I said, 'A quarter?' He said, 'Whatever you wish, but if you increase it that will be better for you.' I said, 'A half?' He said, 'Whatever you wish, but if you increase it that will be better for you.' I said, 'Two-thirds?' and he replied, 'Whatever you wish, but if you increase it that will be better for you.' I said, 'I will devote all my prayer to you.' He replied, 'Then you will be freed from care and your wrong action will be forgiven.' " (Tirmidhī)

536. Abū Ḥumayd as-Sā'idī ﵁ reported that, "The Companions asked, 'O Messenger of Allah, how should we invoke blessing on you?' He ﷺ said, 'Say,

اللَّهُمَّ صَلِّ عَلَى مُحَمَّدٍ وَأَزْوَاجِهِ وَذُرِّيَّتِهِ كَمَا صَلَّيْتَ عَلَى آلِ إِبْرَاهِيمَ وَبَارِكْ عَلَى مُحَمَّدٍ وَأَزْوَاجِهِ وَذُرِّيَّتِهِ كَمَا بَارَكْتَ عَلَى آلِ إِبْرَاهِيمَ إِنَّكَ حَمِيدٌ مَجِيدٌ

"Allāhumma! Ṣalli 'alā Muḥammadin wa 'alā azwājihī wa dhurrīyyātihī kamā ṣallayta 'alā 'āli Ibrāhīma, wa bārik 'alā Muḥammadin wa 'alā azwājihī wa dhurriyyātihī kamā bārakta 'alā 'āli Ibrāhīma Innaka ḥamīdun majīd – O Allah, bless Muḥammad and his wives and descendants as You blessed the family of Ibrāhīm. Grant blessing to Muḥammad and his wives and

descendants as You granted blessing to the family of Ibrāhīm. You are Praiseworthy, Glorious." ' " (Bukhārī, Muslim)

537. Ka'b ibn 'Ujrah ﷺ said, "The Messenger of Allah ﷺ came out to us and we said, 'Messenger of Allah, we know how to greet you, but how should we invoke blessing on you?' He said, 'Say,

اللَّهُمَّ صَلِّ عَلَى مُحَمَّدٍ وَعَلَى آلِ مُحَمَّدٍ كَمَا صَلَّيْتَ عَلَى إِبْرَاهِيمَ وَعَلَى آلِ إِبْرَاهِيمَ إِنَّكَ حَمِيدٌ مَجِيدٌ اللَّهُمَّ بَارِكْ عَلَى مُحَمَّدٍ وَعَلَى آلِ مُحَمَّدٍ كَمَا بَارَكْتَ عَلَى إِبْرَاهِيمَ وَعَلَى آلِ إِبْرَاهِيمَ إِنَّكَ حَمِيدٌ مَجِيدٌ

"Allāhumma! Ṣalli 'alā Muḥammadin wa 'alā 'āli Muḥammadin kamā ṣallayta 'alā Ibrāhīma wa 'alā 'āli Ibrāhīma Innaka ḥamīdun majīd. Allāhumma! Bārik 'alā Muḥammadin wa 'alā 'āli Muḥammadin kamā bārakta 'alā Ibrāhīma wa 'alā 'āli Ibrāhīma. Innaka ḥamidun majīd – O Allah, bless Muḥammad and the family of Muḥammad as You blessed Ibrāhīm and the family of Ibrāhīm. You are Praiseworthy, Glorious. O Allah, grant blessing to Muḥammad and the family of Muḥammad as You granted blessing to Ibrāhīm and the family of Ibrāhīm. You are Praiseworthy, Glorious." ' " (Bukhārī, Muslim)

538. Ibn Mas'ūd ﷺ said, "When you invoke blessing on Allah's Messenger ﷺ, you should invoke the blessing in the best form for you do not know whether that would be shown to him." The people present said, "So teach us." He said, "Say:

اللَّهُمَّ اجْعَلْ صَلاَتَكَ وَرَحْمَتَكَ وَبَرَكَاتِكَ عَلَى سَيِّدِ الْمُرْسَلِينَ وَإِمَامِ الْمُتَّقِينَ وَخَاتَمِ النَّبِيِّينَ مُحَمَّدٍ عَبْدِكَ وَرَسُولِكَ إِمَامِ الْخَيْرِ وَقَائِدِ الْخَيْرِ وَرَسُولِ الرَّحْمَةِ اللَّهُمَّ ابْعَثْهُ مَقَامًا مَحْمُودًا يَغْبِطُهُ بِهِ الأَوَّلُونَ وَالآخِرُونَ اللَّهُمَّ صَلِّ عَلَى مُحَمَّدٍ وَعَلَى آلِ مُحَمَّدٍ كَمَا صَلَّيْتَ عَلَى إِبْرَاهِيمَ وَعَلَى آلِ إِبْرَاهِيمَ إِنَّكَ حَمِيدٌ مَجِيدٌ اللَّهُمَّ بَارِكْ عَلَى مُحَمَّدٍ وَعَلَى آلِ مُحَمَّدٍ كَمَا بَارَكْتَ عَلَى إِبْرَاهِيمَ وَعَلَى آلِ إِبْرَاهِيمَ إِنَّكَ حَمِيدٌ مَجِيدٌ

'Allāhumma! Ij'al ṣalātaka wa raḥmataka wa barakātika 'alā sayyidi'l-mursalīna, wa imāmi'l-muttaqīna, wa khātamin-nabīyyīna Muḥammadin 'abdika wa rasūlika Imāmi'l-khayri wa qā'idi'l-khayri wa rasūli'r-raḥmati. Allāhumma! Ib'athhu maqāman maḥmūdan yaghbiṭuhū bihi'l-awwalūna

wa'l-'ākhirūna. Allāhumma! Ṣalli 'alā Muḥammadin wa 'alā 'āli Muḥammadin kamā ṣallayta 'alā Ibrāhīma wa 'alā 'āli Ibrāhīma Innaka ḥamīdun majīd. Allāhumma! Bārik 'alā Muḥammadin wa 'alā 'āli Muḥammadin kamā bārakta 'alā Ibrāhīma wa 'alā 'āli Ibrāhīma Innaka ḥamīdun majīd – O Allah! Grant Your blessings, mercy and graces to the master of Messengers, the leader of the righteous, the seal of the prophets, Muḥammad, Your slave and Messenger, the leader of good, the commander of good and the Messenger of mercy. O Allah! Raise him up to a praiseworthy station for which he will be envied by the people who came before and after him ﷺ. O Allah! Bless Muḥammad and the household of Muḥammad, as you have blessed Ibrāhīm and the household of Ibrāhīm, You are Praiseworthy, Glorious. O Allah! Show grace to Muḥammad and the household of Muḥammad, as you have shown grace to Ibrāhīm and the household of Ibrāhīm, You are Praiseworthy, Glorious.' " (Ibn Mājah)

The humble compiler 'Abdu'l-Ḥayy ibn Fakhru'd-Dīn ibn 'Abdu'l-'Alī al-Ḥasanī states: 'I completed this collection of *Aḥādīth* at Lucknow on Friday 14th Dhu'l Ḥijjah 1334 AH. There is no might nor strength except by Allah, the Exalted, the Magnificent and may Allah bless our Master and Guardian Muḥammad, his family and his Companions and grant them peace.

The revision of this book was completed on Friday, in the month of Ramaḍān 1391 AH and all Praise belongs to Allah at the Beginning and the End – **Abu'l Ḥasan 'Alī Nadwī.**

SUBJECT INDEX

Subjects are listed according to *Ḥadīth* number; those numbers preceded by 'p' refer to Qur'ānic references mentioned on that page

ALLAH
all are slaves of - 14
ask for needs - 8
be fearful of - 28
best Guardian - 416
bounty of - 427
call on - 17
depend on - 415; 418
elevates the humble - 146
fear - 54; p57; 93; p102; p113; 132; 138; 248; 290; 291; 421; 500
glory be to - 11
he who Allah loves - 40
helps those who are defamed - 105
His love is mandatory - 80
His right on His slave - 2
least in need of a partner - 22
looks at hearts - 25
love - p15; 35; 38
loves constant action - 427
loves to see token of His blessing - 321
Master is - 14
mercy of - 275; 397
names of - 475
only accepts sincere intention - 19
only Allah knows - 3
provides - 4
revenge for sake of - 357
seeking the face of - 21
swear by - 15
those whom Allah will shade - 83
those whom will be shown no mercy - 274
trust in - p111; 414
what Allah decrees - 7
will of - 5
will punish - 282
worship - 198; 378

ANIMALS AND BIRDS
Allah provides for birds - 418
curse on brander of donkey - 288
do not drink like the camel - 312
hearts of birds - 417
kindness to animals - 365
kindness to birds and ants - 289
kindness to camel - 290; 291; 292
mercy to ants - p81
mercy to birds and beasts - 284
mercy to dogs - 283
punishment for not feeding cat - 285
rights of animals and reptiles - 292
tying up animals to be shot - 287
using live creatures as targets - 286

GOOD QUALITIES